A WOMAN'S BOOK *of* DAYS

A WOMAN'S

BOOK of DAYS

BEVERLY WETTENSTEIN

CROWN PUBLISHERS, INC. NEW YORK

Dedicated to my supportive parents, loyal friends, the pioneer women leaders of the past,
present, and future, and a few good mentors.

Published by Crown Publishers, Inc., 201 East 50th Street, New York, New York 10022.
Member of the Crown Publishing Group.

Random House, Inc. New York, Toronto, London, Sydney, Auckland

CROWN is a trademark of Crown Publishers, Inc.

Manufactured in Singapore

Picture Research: Diane Cook
Design: Louise Fili
Design Assistant: Leah Lococo

ISBN 0-517-59700-4

10 9 8 7 6 5 4 3 2 1

First Edition

A *Woman's Book of Days* was written to enlighten, entertain, and inspire women of all ages. It has been specially designed for you to create a permanent diary of important birthdays and personal moments, alongside those of more than one thousand remarkable women leaders from the past up to the present.

You'll discover a treasury of "firsts" for women, plus birthdays, achievements, and milestones, accompanied by a visual tribute in photos and artwork. The journal is rich in little-known facts about popular personalities, as well as many unsung heroines not found in any traditional histories. Whether you choose to climb the corporate ladder or Mt. Everest, hopefully this daily homage to courageous women will encourage you to explore unchartered frontiers.

Celebrate women every day, of every year. These uncommon women of vision and valor have triumphed to redefine a woman's place today—at home, at work, at play—and made society a better place. As Abigail Adams wrote to her husband, John, in 1776, "Remember the Ladies."

J A N U A R Y

1752: Betsy Ross, b. Philadelphia. In 1777 she creates the American flag. 1931: Marlene Sanders, b. Cleveland, Ohio. First woman anchor, TV network evening news (1964); first woman VP, TV network news (1976). 1936: Eve Queler, b. New York City. First woman associate conductor, Metropolitan Orchestra (1965). 1990: Anna Quindlen begins writing Op-Ed column for *The New York Times*; she is awarded the Pulitzer Prize for commentary in 1992. 1993: The Year of the Woman.

New Year's Day

1861: Helen Herron Taft, b. Cincinnati, Ohio. First Lady, 1909–1913, and the first to attend cabinet meetings. She persuades the mayor of Tokyo to donate cherry trees to Washington, D.C. 1994: Nancy Cole becomes the first woman president of Educational Testing Service, which creates the SAT college admission test.

1793: Lucretia Coffin Mott, b. Nantucket, Mass. With Elizabeth Cady Stanton, she organizes the first women's rights convention in Seneca Falls, N.Y. (1848). 1879: Grace Anne Goodhue Coolidge, b. Burlington, Vt. First Lady, 1923–1929. "Being wife to a government worker is a very confining position." 1900: Dorothy Arzner, b. San Francisco. Only woman film director, 1920s–1940s. 1934: Carla Hills, b. Los Angeles. Third woman in U.S. cabinet; first woman secretary of the Dept. of Housing and Urban Development (HUD) (1975–1977). 1936: Betty Rollin, b. New York City. Author, broadcaster.

Opposite: Dorothy Arzner *Right:* Betsy Ross

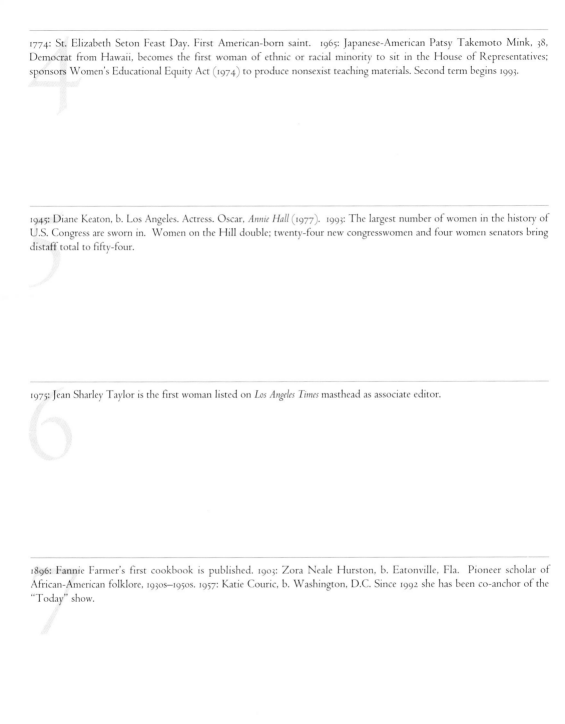

1774: St. Elizabeth Seton Feast Day. First American-born saint. **1965:** Japanese-American Patsy Takemoto Mink, 38, Democrat from Hawaii, becomes the first woman of ethnic or racial minority to sit in the House of Representatives; sponsors Women's Educational Equity Act (1974) to produce nonsexist teaching materials. Second term begins 1993.

1945: Diane Keaton, b. Los Angeles. Actress. Oscar, *Annie Hall* (1977). **1993:** The largest number of women in the history of U.S. Congress are sworn in. Women on the Hill double; twenty-four new congresswomen and four women senators bring distaff total to fifty-four.

1975: Jean Sharley Taylor is the first woman listed on *Los Angeles Times* masthead as associate editor.

1896: Fannie Farmer's first cookbook is published. **1903:** Zora Neale Hurston, b. Eatonville, Fla. Pioneer scholar of African-American folklore, 1930s–1950s. **1957:** Katie Couric, b. Washington, D.C. Since 1992 she has been co-anchor of the "Today" show.

1867: Emily G. Balch, b. Boston. Social worker, labor leader, is second American women to win Nobel Peace Prize (1946). She won because she cofounded the Women's International League for Peace and Freedom. 1909: Evelyn N. Wood, b. Logan, Utah. In 1959 she founds the Reading Dynamics speed reading course. 1939: Carolina Herrera, b. Venezuela. Fashion designer 1981 to present. 1975: Ella Grasso, 56, becomes the first woman governor (D-Conn.) not succeeding her husband. 1977: Pauli Murray, 67, becomes the first African-American woman ordained a priest in two hundred-year-old Protestant Episcopal Church.

1859: Carrie Lane Chapman Catt, b. Ripon, Wis. With Susan B. Anthony, she wins the vote for women. In 1920 she organizes the League of Women Voters. 1875: Gertrude Vanderbilt Whitney, b. New York City. In 1931 the sculptor becomes first woman founder of a major art museum, New York City's Whitney Museum of Art. 1877: Jane Newell Blair, b. Joplin, Mo. VP, Democratic National Committee; only woman officer (1924). 1886: Ida Cohen Rosenthal, b. Russia. The founder in 1923 of Maidenform, Inc., she creates the modern bra, the first using cup sizes. In the thirties, *Time* notes she "probably had a greater impact on the U.S. female form than all the couturiers in Paris." 1908: Simone de Beauvoir, b. Paris. She attacks the inferior role of women in *The Second Sex* (1949). 1928: Judith (Tarcher) Krantz, b. New York City. Best-selling author.

Left: Zora Neale Hurston *Right:* Gertrude Vanderbilt Whitney

1878: Women's suffrage amendment is introduced and defeated in the Senate; until its passage in 1920, it is reintroduced in each succeeding Congress. **1972:** *Ms.* magazine debuts as a special preview section in *New York* magazine.

1895: Alice Paul, b. Morristown, N.Y. Drafts and has introduced in Congress the first national Equal Rights Amendment for women (1923). **1921:** First women jurors are sworn in at the Old Bailey in London. **1921:** Juanita Kreps, b. Lynch, Ky. First woman secretary of the Dept. of Commerce (1977–1979); first woman director, N.Y. Stock Exchange (1972).

1820: Caroline Severance, b. New York City. With Susan B. Anthony, creates Equal Rights Assn. (1866). At 91, she is first woman to register to vote in Calif.

1850: Charlotte Ray, b. New York City. First African-American woman lawyer, she practices in the District of Columbia (1872). **1975:** Margaret Wilson, 56, is elected the first African-American woman chairperson of the NAACP, which was founded in 1910.

1858: Hannah Greenebaum Solomon, b. Chicago. Founder, first president, National Council of Jewish Women (1893). **1941:** Faye Dunaway, b. Bascom, Fla. Actress. Oscar, *Network* (1976). **1972:** Queen Margrethe II, 32, becomes first woman to rule Denmark.

1845: Ella Flag Young, b. Buffalo, N.Y. First woman superintendent of major public school system, Chicago, 1909–1915. First woman president, National Education Assn. (1910). **1878:** Women receive degrees for first time at London Univ. **1939:** Mrs. Ruth Wakefield invents chocolate-chip cookies at Toll House Inn in Whitman, Mass. Mrs. (Debbi) Fields will open her first "Chocolate Chippery" cookie store in Palo Alto, Calif. in 1977; today, there are almost eight hundred stores worldwide. **1971:** The National Press Club in Washington, D.C. votes to admit women members. Vivian Vahlberg of *The Daily Oklahoman* is elected the first woman president in 1982.

Martin Luther King, Jr.'s Birthday

1978: Six women astronauts qualify for U.S. space program—the first time in NASA's eighteen years of operation.

1922: Betty White, b. Oak Park, Ill. Actress. **1934:** Shari Lewis, b. New York City. Puppeteer.

1949: Brooks Brothers, established in 1818, introduces women's pink oxford button-down shirt.

18

Maya Angelou

19 1905: Oveta Culp Hobby, b. Killeen, Tex. Second woman in U.S. Cabinet (twenty years after Frances Perkins); first secretary of the Dept. of Health, Education, and Welfare (HEW) (1953–1955). 1945: Dolly Parton, b. Sevierville, Tenn., the fourth of twelve children. Singer, songwriter, actress. In 1989 she will buy the radio station where she first performed. 1966: Indira Gandhi is elected prime minister of India; serves 1966–1977, 1978–1984; assassinated by Sikhs.

20 1879: Ruth St. Denis, b. Newark, N.J. First lady of American dance; Martha Graham is a student. 1925: Miriam Amanda Ferguson becomes first U.S. woman governor, Tex. 1993: Maya Angelou, 65, delivers Pres. Bill Clinton's inauguration poem, "On the Pulse of Morning." Opera singer Marilyn Horne, 59, performs. Pres. Clinton appoints women to six of twenty-two cabinet positions.

Ruth St. Denis

1957: Geena Davis, b. Wareham, Mass. Actress. Oscar, *The Accidental Tourist* (1988).

1973: Sarah Weddington, 28, wins *Roe* v. *Wade* in the U.S. Supreme Court. Court rules that a state must guarantee women the right of reproductive choice to terminate an unwanted pregnancy during the first six months. 1991: U.S. Supreme Court rules Princeton's remaining all-male eating club must admit women members.

1918: Gertrude B. Elion, b. New York City. Recieves Nobel Prize for Medicine (1988). First woman, National Inventor's Hall of Fame, for creation of new drugs (1991). 1933: Chita Rivera, b. Washington, D.C. Actress and dancer. Receives Tony at 61 for *Kiss of the Spider Woman*. 1957: Princess Caroline, b. Monaco.

1862: Edith Wharton, b. New York City. First woman to receive Pulitzer Prize twice: for Fiction, *The Age of Innocence* (1921) and for Drama, *The Old Maid* (1935). 1866: Dr. Mary Walker is the first and only woman to receive a Congressional Medal of Honor for her medical work in the Civil War. 1888: Neysa McMein, b. Quincy, Ill. She will be the first woman artist invited to paint portraits of presidents (Hoover and Harding). Designs all McCall's covers, 1923-37; creates "Betty Crocker" image. 1927: Paula Fickes Hawkins, b. Salt Lake City. First woman elected to the Senate in her own right; from 1980 to 1987 she serves as a Republican from Fla. 1968: Mary Lou Retton, b. Fairmont, W.Va. Gymnast is first and only American woman to win gold medal in all-around gymnastics competition at the Olympics; also awarded one silver, two bronze medals (1984). First woman on Wheaties box. 1985: Penny Eileen Harrington becomes the first big-city police department chief, in Portland, Oreg. She is promoted after twenty-two years on the force. Each promotion followed her filing a complaint.

1871: Maud Wood Park, b. Boston. First national president, League of Women Voters (1919). Cofounder, Parent Teacher Assn. 1882: Virginia (Stephen) Woolf, b. London. Novelist, *A Room of One's Own* (1929). "A woman must have money and a room of her own." 1933: Corazon Aquino, b. Philippines. Philippines president, 1986–1992.

Virginia Woolf

1872: Julia Morgan, b. San Francisco. First woman graduate, Univ. Calif., engineering (1894). First woman licensed architect, Calif. Phoebe Hearst helps her secure early commissions. From 1920 to 1938 she designs W.R. Hearst's San Simeon. 1893: Bessie Coleman, b. Atlanta, Tex. "Brave Bessie" becomes the first licensed African-American woman pilot in world. First U.S. woman to earn international pilot's license, 1921. She will be thrown from open cockpit during exhibition flight and die at 33. 1905: Maria Augusta von Trapp, b. Vienna, Austria. Her life story will inspire *The Sound of Music* (1959).

1944: Mairead Corrigan, b. Belfast, Northern Ireland. Nobel Peace Prize (1976). Cofounder, Northern Ireland's Peace People movement, created after three of her sister's children are killed in a shoot-out.

1873: Colette (Gabrielle Claudine), b. France. Author, actress. Second woman in the French Legion of Honor. 1933: Susan Sontag, b. New York City. Author, critic.

1881: Alice Evans, b. Neath, Pa. First woman scientist, U.S. Dairy Div. (1913). Discovers danger of unpasteurized milk; pasteurization will be required by the thirties. 1939: Germaine Greer, b. Australia. Author, *The Female Eunuch* (1970), early feminist book. 1954: Oprah Winfrey, b. Kosciusko, Miss. First woman to own and produce her own nationally syndicated talk show; first African-American, third woman (after Mary Pickford, Lucille Ball) to own movie and TV production studio; produces work of women writers. Oscar nominee, *The Color Purple* (1985). Successfully lobbied for The National Child Abuse Protection Act (the "Oprah bill") to establish database of convicted child abusers (1993). Donates millions for education, abused children, and battered women.

1912: Barbara W. Tuchman, b. New York City. First woman to win Pulitzer Prize for General Nonfiction, *The Guns of August* (1963); second Pulitzer, *Stilwell and the American Experience in China* (1972). 1937: Vanessa Redgrave, b. London. Actress. 1944: Sharon Pratt Dixon, b. Washington, D.C. First woman mayor of Washington, D.C. (1990).

1885: Anna Pavlova, b. Russia. Dancer. 1923: Carol Channing, b. Seattle. Actress. Tony, *Hello Dolly* (1964).

Oprah Winfrey

1878: Hattie Wyatt Caraway, b. Bakerville, Tenn. First woman elected to U.S. Senate and the first to preside over the Senate (1932); first woman reelected senator (1938). 1918: Muriel Spark, b. Edinburgh, Scotland. Novelist, *The Prime of Miss Jean Brodie* (1961). 1971: Princess Stephanie, b. Monaco. 1981: Gro Harlem Bruntland is elected Norway's first woman prime minister and reelected in 1986. At 42, she was the youngest woman to head a modern government.

1841: Sarah Hackett Stevenson, b. Buffalo Grove, Ill. First woman member of the American Medical Assn. (1876). By 1992, the AMA has 119,000 women members. 1881: Anne Bauchens, b. St. Louis. Sole editor for Cecile B. De Mille's last forty films, 1918–1959. Three Oscar nominations: *Cleopatra* (1934); *The Greatest Show on Earth* (1952); *The Ten Commandments* (1956, at age 75). 1905: Ayn Rand, b. St. Petersburg, Russia. Author. "Money is the root of all good." *The Fountainhead* (1943); *Atlas Shrugged* (1957). 1923: Liz Smith, b. Ft. Worth, Tex. Syndicated columnist.

1821: Elizabeth Blackwell, b. Bristol, England. In 1849 she becomes the first licensed woman graduate of a medical school, Geneva Medical College, N.Y. She organizes the first hospital in the world with an all-woman staff, including interns, the New York Infirmary for Women and Children. In 1868, with her sister, Dr. Emily Blackwell, she establishes the Women's Medical College of the New York Infirmary, the first for women. She becomes the first woman in the British medical register (1859) and, in conjunction, with Florence Nightingale, she opens Women's Medical College in England. 1874: Gertrude Stein, b. Allegheny, Pa. Author leads expatriate "Lost Generation" in 1920s Paris. 1946: Linda J. Wachner, b. New York City. At Warnaco in 1993 she is the highest-paid U.S. woman CEO, with a salary of $3.2 million. One of three women CEOs on *Business Week*'s 1,000 "Corporate Elite" list (the sole woman listed, 1986), she is the only woman to successfully win a hostile corporate takeover.

Opposite: Gertrude Stein *Right:* Elizabeth Blackwell

1913: Rosa Parks, b. Tuskegee, Ala. "Mother of civil rights movement." In 1955, the 42-year-old seamstress refuses to surrender her seat on a segregated Montgomery, Ala., bus, is arrested and fined. This leads to Dr. Martin Luther King's bus boycott, which lasts 382 days until the Supreme Court mandates integrated buses. 1921: Betty (Goldstein) Friedan, b. Peoria, Ill. A founder of the modern women's rights movement. After a decade as a wife and mother, sends a questionnaire to her Smith College 1942 classmates. The results are published in the best-seller *The Feminine Mystique* (1963). Founds National Organization for Women (NOW) in 1966, to lobby for women's rights and child care; president until 1970. Also author of *The Second Stage* (1982); *The Fountain of Age* (1993). 1931: Isabelle Perón, b. Argentina. First woman president in Argentina; succeeds husband, 1974–1976; ousted in coup.

1931: Two hundred women, including Dorothy Shaver, Elizabeth Arden, Helena Rubenstein, and Eleanor Roosevelt, attend the Fashion Group's first meeting in New York City. By 1993 membership worldwide exceeds 7,000. 1939: Jane Bryant Quinn, b. Niagara Falls, N.Y. Financial columnist. 1989: Judith Richards Hope becomes the first woman elected to 353-year-old Harvard Corporation's chief governing board.

1883: Christine McGaffrey, b. Boston. Founds League of Advertising Women (Advertising Women of N.Y.) in 1912, because no advertising organization admitted women. Conducts one of first surveys on women's buying habits. 1893: Madge Thurlow Macklin, b. Philadelphia. Pioneer physician and geneticist is instrumental in having genetics incorporated into medical school curricula. In 1938 only one medical school has a genetics course; by 1953, 55% of U.S. medical schools recognize genetics. 1950: Natalie Cole, b. Los Angeles. "Unforgettable" singer.

1867: Laura Ingalls Wilder, b. Pepin, Wis. At 65, begins writing Little House books. By 1977, twenty million copies are sold; TV series 1974–1982.

1944: Alice Walker, b. Eatonton, Ga., youngest of eight children. First African-American woman to win Pulitzer Prize for Fiction, *The Color Purple* (1983). At eight she is blinded in one eye.

Alice Walker

1819: Lydia Pinkham, b. Lynn, Mass. She manufactures patent medicine, "Mrs. Lydia E. Pinkham's Vegetable Compound," on her cellar kitchen stove (1875). It promises a "positive cure for all those complaints and weaknesses so common to our female population." By 1898 it is the most advertised product in U.S. and hers becomes the best-known face of the nineteenth century. Her health book sells more than one million copies. 1874: Amy Lowell, b. Brookline, Mass. Poet. 1926: Letitia Baldrige, b. Miami Beach, Fla. *Time* calls her "America's leading arbiter of manners."

MRS. LYDIA E. PINKHAM, OF LYNN, MASS.,

Woman can Sympathize with Woman.

Health of Woman is the Hope of the Race.

Yours for Health

Lydia E. Pinkham

LYDIA E. PINKHAM'S
VEGETABLE COMPOUND.
Is a Positive Cure

1927: Leontyne Price, b. Laurel, Miss. First international American opera star; "*Prima Donna Assoluta*" (first lady of opera). Has sung with the Metropolitan Opera since 1961.

1925: Virginia Johnson, b. Springfield, Mo. Pioneer sex therapist, coauthor, landmark *Human Sexual Response* (1966). 1934: Mary Quant, b. London. British fashion designer. "Mother of the Miniskirt" pioneers mid-1950s/1960s Chelsea Girl look. 1988: Boy Scouts of America vote to end requirement that troop leaders must be male.

Leontyne Price

1938: Judy Blume, b. Elizabeth, N.J. Children's book author. 1989: Right Rev. Barbara Harris, an African-American, becomes the first woman and 834th Anglican bishop of the diocese of Mass.

Lincoln's Birthday

1827: Sister Julia (Susan McGroarty), b. Ireland. Founds Trinity College in Washington, D.C., in 1900, to provide higher education for Catholic women. 1885: Bess Wallace Truman, b. Independence, Mo. First Lady, 1945–1953. Installs air-conditioning in the White House, which she calls the "Great White Jail." 1908: Pauline Frederick, b. Gallitzin, Pa. First woman network radio and TV correspondent (1939). First woman to cover national political convention (1948). First woman moderator, presidential debate, between Gerald R. Ford and Jimmy Carter (1976).

In 1840, Esther Howland originates the printed valentine in America. 1838: Margaret Knight, b. York, Maine. At 30, the "woman Edison" invents first square-bottomed brown-paper grocery bag and earns her first patent (1870). She aquires twenty-five more patents but sells them to her employer for cash and never profits from her inventions. 1941: Donna E. Shalala, b. Cleveland, Ohio. Secretary of the Dept. of Health and Human Services, 1993 to present. First woman chancellor, Univ. of Wis.; president, Hunter College, New York City.

Valentine's Day

1820: Susan B. Anthony, b. Adams, Mass. Cofounder, National Woman Suffrage Assn. (1869). In 1872, she and twelve women are arrested, fined $100, which she refuses to pay, and convicted for voting in presidential election—a criminal act by a woman. When she dies in 1906, only four states have granted women the vote, yet her final words are "Failure is impossible." 1879: Pres. Rutherford B. Hayes signs bill ruling that women attorneys with three years' experience before a state supreme court may argue cases before the U.S. Supreme Court. Belva Lockwood, who lobbied for the bill, became the first woman lawyer admitted that year.

1989: Rebecca Sinkler becomes the first woman editor of *The New York Times Book Review*, founded in 1911. 1991: Judy Sweet is the first woman president of the National Collegiate Athletic Assn. (NCAA). In 1975 she was the first woman to administer a joint men's and women's athletic program, at the Univ. of Calif., San Diego. 1993: Judit Polgar, 16, of Hungary, beats former world chess champion Boris Spassky, 56, in a ten-game match. Youngest player to win the rank of international grandmaster (1992). 1994: Oscar, Emmy, and Grammy award-winning lyricist Marilyn Bergman is elected the first woman president of ASCAP (American Society of Composers, Authors & Publishers), founded in 1914. Oscar, Golden Globe Award, *The Windmills of Your Mind* (1968); Oscar, *Yentl* (1983).

1879: Dorothy Canfield Fisher, b. Lawrence, Kans. Novelist is appointed to Book-of-the-Month Club's first board of selection in 1926; only woman on board for twenty-five years.

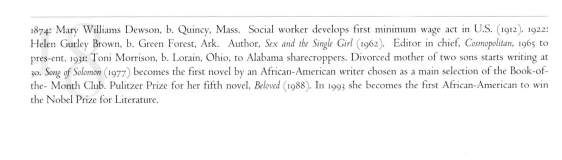

1874: Mary Williams Dewson, b. Quincy, Mass. Social worker develops first minimum wage act in U.S. (1912). 1922: Helen Gurley Brown, b. Green Forest, Ark. Author, *Sex and the Single Girl* (1962). Editor in chief, *Cosmopolitan*, 1965 to present. 1931: Toni Morrison, b. Lorain, Ohio, to Alabama sharecroppers. Divorced mother of two sons starts writing at 30. *Song of Solomon* (1977) becomes the first novel by an African-American writer chosen as a main selection of the Book-of-the- Month Club. Pulitzer Prize for her fifth novel, *Beloved* (1988). In 1993 she becomes the first African-American to win the Nobel Prize for Literature.

1867: Annie Nathan Meyer, b. New York City. Cofounder, trustee, of Barnard College. When she learns that women take exams at Columbia College that include questions from lectures they are barred from attending, she decides to raise funds to open a fully accredited affiliated women's college: Barnard. It opens in 1889.

1966: Cindy Crawford, b. DeKalb, Ill. Model, broadcaster, entrepreneur.

1855: Alice Freeman Palmer, b. Binghamton N.Y. Founder and president, American Assn. of University Women (1882). President, Wellesley College, 1882. 1927: Erma (Fiste) Bombeck, b. Dayton, Ohio. At 37, the suburban housewife and mother of three begins writing for local weekly. By 1990, syndicated column reaches thirty million readers worldwide. "Know the difference between success and fame. Success is Mother Teresa. Fame is Madonna." 1936: Barbara Jordan, b. Houston, Tex. First African-American congresswoman from Deep South, Tex. (1972); member of House Judiciary Committee during Nixon impeachment hearings. Delivers keynote address to Democratic National Convention (1976, 1992). Chair, U.S. Commission on Immigration Reform, 1993 to present. 1947: Rep. Olympia J. Snowe, b. Augusta, Maine. Republican, Maine; eighth term, 1993 to present. Cochair, with Rep. Patricia Schroeder, of Congressional Caucus for Women's Issues.

1889: Lady Olave St. Claire Baden-Powell, b. England, In 1902, founds International Girl Scout Movement. 1892: Edna St. Vincent Millay, b. Rockland, Maine. Poet is considered "spokesman for the human spirit." First woman to receive Pulitzer Prize for Poetry (1923), *Ballad of the Harp-Weaver*, her fourth book of verse.

Washington's Birthday

1787: Emma Hart Willard, b. Berlin, Conn. At 27, she founds Middlebury Female Seminary, the first higher education institution for women, in her home. She moves to Troy, N.Y., and in 1895 the school is renamed the Emma Willard School. 1901: Ruth Nichols, b. New York City. Achieves thirty-five "firsts" for women in aviation. First woman commercial pilot for passenger airline (1932).

1912: Henrietta Szold, 52, founds Hadassah, now the world's largest (385,000 members) and oldest women's Zionist organization, focusing on health care and education in U.S. and Israel. Between 1992 and 1993, Hadassah raises $77.5 million through volunteer activities. 1956: Paula Zahn, b. Omaha, Neb. Broadcaster; co-anchor, "CBS Morning News."

1905: Adelle Davis, b. Lizton, Ind. In 1972, *Time* names her "the high priestess of a new nutrition religion." 1943: Sally Jessy Raphael, b. Easton, Pa. First nationally syndicated woman TV talk show host debuts on October 16, 1983; her program is still broadcast.

Marian Anderson

1994: Margaret Carlson is *Time* magazine's first woman columnist in its seventy-year history. 1994: J. Veronica Biggins becomes the first African-American director of presidential personnel at the White House.

1850: Laura Elizabeth Howe Richards, b. Boston. With her sister, Maud Howe Elliott, wins Pulitzer Prize for biography of her mother, Julia Ward Howe ("The Battle Hymn of the Republic") (1915). 1869: Alice Hamilton, b. New York City. Harvard's first woman professor, at the medical school (1919). 1902: Marian Anderson, b. Philadelphia. Arturo Toscanini remarks in 1935 at Salzburg, "What I heard today one is privileged to hear only once in a hundred years." First African-American singer to appear at Metropolitan Opera (1955–1965). Goodwill ambassador and delegate to UN (1958). 1930: Joanne Woodward, b. Thomasville, Ga. At 27, wins Oscar for third film, *The Three Faces of Eve* (1957). 1932: Elizabeth Taylor, b. London. Oscars: *Butterfield 8* (1960); *Who's Afraid of Virginia Woolf?* (1967). Cofounder (1985) and currently chair, American Foundation for AIDS Research. 1942: Charlayne Hunter Gault, b. Due West, S.C. In 1961 she was the first African-American woman to desegregate Univ. of Ga. since its commencement 176 years before. News correspondent, "MacNeil/Lehrer NewsHour," 1978 to present.

1797: Mary Mason Lyon, b. Buckland, Mass. Founder and principal, Mt. Holyoke Female Seminary, South Hadley, Mass.; first independent institution of higher learning for women in U.S., opens in 1837 with eighty students; 400 are turned away; in 1895 it becomes Mt. Holyoke College. 1991: Rhaleda Zia, widow of Pres. Rahman of Bangladesh, wins free election.

1892: Augusta Christine Savage, b. Green Grove Springs, Fla. In 1939 she is one of four women and the only African-American woman invited to produce sculpture for World's Fair in New York City. President, Salon of Contemporary Negro Art (1939); first U.S. gallery devoted to African-American artists.

Leap Year

MARCH

1864: Rebecca Lee becomes the first African-American woman in the U.S. to receive a medical degree, from New England Medical College, Boston. **1917:** Dinah Shore, b. Winchester, Tenn. Awarded eight Emmys, the most for any performer. **1978:** "Women's History Week" is first observed in Sonoma, Calif. **1987:** Congressional resolution naming National Women's History Month is passed.

1987: Young women take top two prizes in Westinghouse Science Talent Search: Louise Chang, 17, Univ. Chicago Lab. School, wins first prize, and Elizabeth Wilmer, Stuyvesant HS, New York City, wins second prize.

1962: Jackie Joyner-Kersee, b. East St. Louis, Ill. Considered the world's greatest female athlete. Despite asthma, she wins two gold medals in the 1988 Olympics and one gold and bronze medal in the 1992 Olympics. Establishes community foundation to maintain recreation centers for disadvantaged youth.

1982: Bertha Wilson is the first woman appointed to Canada's Supreme Court.

Jackie Joyner-Kersee

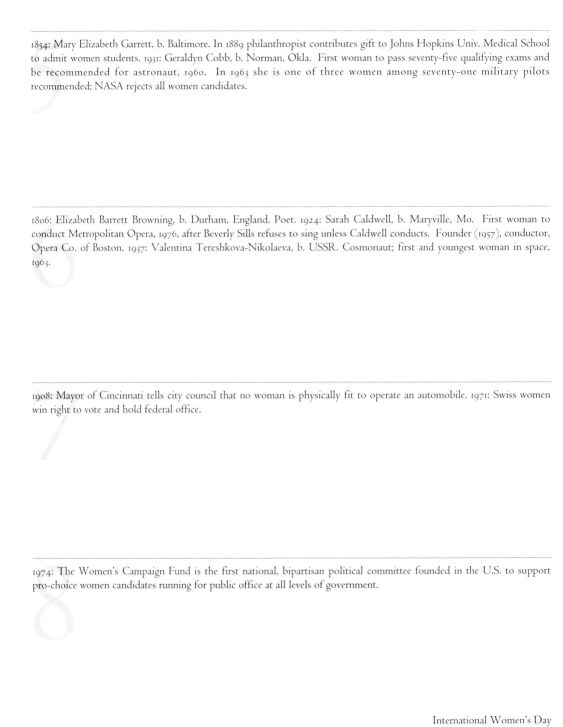

1854: Mary Elizabeth Garrett, b. Baltimore. In 1889 philanthropist contributes gift to Johns Hopkins Univ. Medical School to admit women students. 1931: Geraldyn Cobb, b. Norman, Okla. First woman to pass seventy-five qualifying exams and be recommended for astronaut, 1960. In 1963 she is one of three women among seventy-one military pilots recommended; NASA rejects all women candidates.

1806: Elizabeth Barrett Browning, b. Durham, England. Poet. 1924: Sarah Caldwell, b. Maryville, Mo. First woman to conduct Metropolitan Opera, 1976, after Beverly Sills refuses to sing unless Caldwell conducts. Founder (1957), conductor, Opera Co. of Boston. 1937: Valentina Tereshkova-Nikolaeva, b. USSR. Cosmonaut; first and youngest woman in space, 1963.

1908: Mayor of Cincinnati tells city council that no woman is physically fit to operate an automobile. 1971: Swiss women win right to vote and hold federal office.

1974: The Women's Campaign Fund is the first national, bipartisan political committee founded in the U.S. to support pro-choice women candidates running for public office at all levels of government.

International Women's Day

1928: Peggy Charen, b. New York City. Founder, Action for Children's Television (ACT), 1969–1992. In 1990 champions Children's Television Act. 1990: Marianne Spraggins, working at Smith Barney, becomes the first and only African-American woman managing director in investment banking.

1867: Lillian D. Wald, b. Cincinnati, Ohio. In 1883 the sociologist founds Henry St. Settlement, New York City. Founder of Foreign Policy Assn. 1969: The National Women's Hall of Fame is founded in Seneca Falls, N.Y., site of the first Women's Rights Convention.

Sarah Caldwell

1849: Eliza Nicholson, b. Hancock County, Miss. First woman newspaper publisher in the South, *New Orleans Times Picayune*. 1903: Dorothy Schiff, b. New York City. First woman newspaper publisher, the *New York Post* (1942).

1877: Annette Abbott Adams, b. Prattville, Calif. In 1912 she is the only woman law graduate from Univ. Calif., Berkeley. First woman federal prosecutor (1914); first woman assistant attorney general (1920); first woman on Calif. Supreme Court (1950). 1910: Camp Fire Girls is founded. 1946: Liza Minnelli, b. Los Angeles. Actress, singer. 1993: Janet Reno, 55, is sworn in as the first woman U.S. attorney general. She worked her way through Harvard Law School, where she was one of sixteen women in a class of five hundred that graduated in 1963. 1994: The Church of England ordains thirty-two woman priests; the first in 460 years of Anglican tradition.

1892: Janet Flanner, b. Indianapolis, Ind. "Paris Letter" correspondent for *The New Yorker*; for thirty years she signed her columns "Genet." 1916: Lindy Boggs, b. Brunswick Plantation, La. Elected U.S. representative in 1973; chairperson of the 1976 Democratic National Convention. A special lounge, known as the Lindy Boggs Women's Reading Room, is created for the seventeen congresswomen sharing one bathroom in 1961. The seven women senators will get a two-stall facility in 1993.

1833: Lucy Hobbs Taylor, b. Franklin City, N.Y. First woman to receive dentistry degree, she graduates from the Ohio College of Dental Surgery in 1866. First woman admitted to a state (Iowa) dental assn. (1865). In 1970 women earn 1% of dental degrees and by 1993, 32%. 1877: Edna Wollman Chase, b. Asbury Park, N.J. Editor in chief, *Vogue*, 1914–1955. Organizes first American fashion show in 1944, following the closing of Paris fashion houses in WWII; promotes American fashion internationally. 1887: Sylvia Woodbridge Beach, b. Baltimore, Md. In 1919 she opens Shakespeare & Co. bookshop in Paris. Publishes James Joyce's *Ullysses* (1922), after American and British publishers reject it. First printing is sold exclusively at her shop. 1923: Diane (Nemerov) Arbus, b. New York City. Photographer.

1907: First women MPs are elected, in Finland. **1933:** Ruth Bader Ginsburg, b. New York City. Appointed in 1993, she is the second woman to sit on the U.S. Supreme Court, after Sandra Day O'Connor. (See Oct. 4.)

1822: Rosa Bonheur, b. Bordeaux, France. In the late 1840s she is one of the world's best animal painters. Emperor Napoleon III refuses to award Legion of Honor to a woman. Empress Eugenie, acting as Regent in his absence, awards it herself (1864). **1886:** Susan Hayhurst becomes the first woman pharmacist in the U.S., graduating from Philadelphia College of Pharmacy. By 1993, women will earn a majority of pharmacy degrees.

1846: Kate Greenaway, b. London. *Mother Goose* illustrator. **1875:** Mary T. Hopkins Norton, b. Jersey City, N.J. In 1925 the first woman Democrat elected to Congress not preceded by husband. By 1932 she is the first to lead state political party. As chair of House Labor Committee, 1932–1947, she is credited with passage of the Fair Labor Standards Act, which bars sex-based salary differentials. **1969:** Golda Meir, 70, becomes Israel's first woman prime minister, serving until she retires in 1974. A teacher in U.S., she stipulates she will marry only if husband immigrates to then Palestine (1921). In 1948, after Israel becomes independent, she is ambassador to Moscow. **1989:** Grand Marshal Dorothy Hayden Cudahy is first woman to lead the 229-year-old St. Patrick's Day parade in New York City.

St. Patrick's Day

1964: Bonnie Blair, b. Champaign, Ill. Speed skater wins hers fifth gold medal, the record for a U.S. woman in the Olympics, and her sixth medal overall, becoming the most successful Winter Olympian in U.S. history (1994). Sprinter Evelyn Ashford, swimmer Janet Evans, and diver Pat McCormick earned four Olympic gold medals.

1868: Senda Berenson, b. Lithuania. Smith College physical education teacher introduces basketball in 1892; in 1901 she introduces field hockey.

1852: Harriet Beecher Stowe's first novel, *Uncle Tom's Cabin*, is published and becomes America's first best-selling million-copy novel. 1951: Nicole Miller, b. Ft. Worth, Tex. Creates signature theme fabric designs; founds own company (1982). 1958: Holly Hunter, b. Atlanta, Ga. Actress. Oscar, *The Piano* (1993).

1905: Phyllis McGinley, b. Ontario, Oreg. Her 1960 Pulitzer Prize for Poetry is the first awarded for light verse.

1977: The National Women's Studies Assn. is established. By 1990, there are 621 programs. Cornell University developed the first women's studies course in 1969. 1994: Lynn Redgrave becomes the first woman president of the exclusive 100-year-old Players Club for performers. Helen Hayes was the first woman inducted, in 1988.

1857: Fannie Farmer, b. Boston. She opens her own school, introduces first standardized level measurements, and the *Boston Cooking School Cook Book* (1896), for which she has to pay production costs. In its first seventy years, sales reach four million copies. 1884: Florence Ellinwood Allen, b. Salt Lake City. First woman to serve as a federal judge (1934–1959). 1897: Margaret Farrar, b. New York City. Coproducer, first crossword puzzle book (1924). Pioneers and edits *New York Times* puzzle column, beginning Sundays in 1942 and daily in 1950. 1924: Bette Nesmith Graham, b. Dallas, Tex. In 1951 she invents Liquid Paper to correct typing errors. She markets it herself after IBM declines to buy it. In 1979, she sells the company to Gillette Corp. for $47.5 million, plus royalties. 1974: Coalition of Labor Union Women is founded by Myra K. Wolfgang in Chicago. 1970: "Women in Revolt," *Newsweek* cover story, sparks revolution internally, resulting in promotions for sixty women staffers.

1912: Dorothy Height, b. Richmond, Va. President, National Council of Negro Women, 1957 to present, representing four million women.

1820: Anne Brontë, b. Yorkshire, England. Her collected poems and those of her sisters, Charlotte and Emily, are issued under pseudonyms at their own expense. 1911: Triangle Shirtwaist Co. fire, New York City, in which 146 immigrant women workers die because they were locked in to curtail thefts. Tragedy leads to enactment of sweatshop laws and fire regulations. 1922: Eileen Ford, b. New York City. Cofounder, in 1946, of a modeling agency. 1925: (Mary) Flannery O'Connor, b. Savannah, Ga. *A Good Man Is Hard to Find, and Other Stories* (1955). 1935: Gloria Steinem, b. Toledo, Ohio. Women's rights activist, cofounder, editor, *Ms.* magazine (1971); Ms. Foundation for Women (1972); cofounder, Coalition of Labor Union Women. Author, *Outrageous Acts and Other Rebellions* (1983); *Revolution from Within: A Book of Self-Esteem* (1991). 1942: Aretha Franklin, b. Memphis, Tenn. "Queen of Soul." 1973: First ten women are elected members of 171-year-old London Stock Exchange.

1863: Bertha Van Hoosen, b. Stony Creek, Mich. Cofounder and first president, American Medical Women's Assn. (1915). Pioneers use of anesthesia in childbirth. 1930: Sandra Day O'Connor, b. El Paso, Tex. First woman to join Supreme Court as justice, on September 25, 1981. She graduated from Stanford third in her class and was *Law Review* editor in 1952. Her only job offer was as legal secretary. She opts for public service. In 1973 she becomes first woman to serve as majority leader in Ariz. Senate. 1944: Diana Ross, b. Detroit, Mich. Actress-singer sells the most number-one hits of any woman.

1924: Sarah Vaughan, b. Newark, N.J. "The Divine" jazz and pop singer wins amateur contest at the Apollo Theater, New York City, in 1943.

Sarah Vaughan

1910: Dorothy Hodgkin, b. Cairo, Egypt. Discovers the structure of insulin. Nobel Prize for Chemistry (1964).

1875: Lou Henry Hoover, b. Waterloo, Iowa. First Lady, 1929–1933. First to deliver a speech over the radio. Only female officer of National Amateur Athletic Federation (1922). 1918: Pearl Bailey, b. Newport News, Va. Jazz singer will become U.S. rep. to UN. 1923: Julia Walsh, b. Akron, Ohio. First woman to purchase a seat on the American Stock Exchange (1965). First woman to graduate from the Harvard Business School's Advanced Management Program (1962).

1888: The National Council of Women of the U.S. is organized by Susan B. Anthony, Clara Barton, Lucy Stone, Julia Ward Howe, and Elizabeth Cady Stanton. 1902: Brooke Astor, b. Portsmouth, N.H. Philanthropist, author, and grande dame of New York City society. As president of The Astor Foundation, since 1959, she has given away $170 million.

1929: Liz Claiborne, b. Brussels. With $200,000 from family and friends, she founds Liz Claiborne, Inc., in 1976. Company goes public and is the second-largest apparel company on the *Fortune* 500 list for 1981. She retires from the company in 1990 and founds an environmental foundation. 1993: Joyce D. Miller becomes executive director, Glass Ceiling Commission of Dept. of Labor, created in 1991 to study barriers that women and minorities face in advancing to senior positions in large companies. First woman elected to AFL-CIO's executive council. President, Coalition of Labor Union Women.

Liz Claiborne

APRIL

1877: Aurelia Henry Reinhardt, b. San Francisco. President, Mills College, 1916–1943. Chair, General Federation of Women's Clubs, 1928–1930. President, AAUW, 1923–1927.

1878: A. T. Stewart opens first hotel exclusively for women in New York City; $7–$12/week, incl. meals. **1917:** Jeannette Rankin, Republican from Montana, 36, is seated as the first woman in U.S. House of Representatives, running on a platform of peace and women's rights, 1917–1919, 1941–1943. Only member to vote against WWI and WWII; defeated in next elections. Authors first bill for government-sponsored instruction in maternity and infant hygiene and supports eight-hour workday. At 87 she leads Jeannette Rankin Brigade of five thousand women to the Capitol to protest Vietnam War. **1931:** Jackie Mitchell, 17, pitches exhibition baseball game against New York Yankees and strikes out Babe Ruth and Lou Gehrig.

1946: Hanna Suchocka, b. Pleszew, Poland. In 1992, she becomes the first woman prime minister of Poland. **1979:** With the largest majority since 1901, Jane Byrne is elected the first woman mayor of Chicago. **1982:** The Committee of 200 is founded to bring preeminent, top-earning entrepreneurial and corporate businesswomen together. By 1993, international membership includes 350 women business leaders.

1887: Susanna Medora, 27, is elected the first woman mayor in Argonia, Kans. **1928:** Maya Angelou, b. St. Louis. She will present Pres. Bill Clinton's inaugural poem, "On the Pulse of Morning" (1993). Author, *I Know Why the Caged Bird Sings*. First African-American woman director in Hollywood. Nightclub, stage, and TV performer. In 1972 she will write the script for *Georgia, Georgia*, the first original screenplay by an African-American woman to be produced. First African-American streetcar conductor, San Francisco. She will hold lifetime position as prof. of American Studies at Wake Forest Univ., Winston-Salem, N.C., beginning in 1981.

Jeannette Rankin

Bette DAVIS

JEZEBEL

with
HENRY FONDA   GEORGE BRENT
MARGARET LINDSAY   DONALD CRISP FAY BAINTER

A WILLIAM WYLER PRODUCTION

A WARNER BROS. PICTURE

1908: Bette Davis, b. Lowell, Mass. First woman president, Academy of Motion Picture Arts & Sciences (1941); first woman, American Film Institute's "Life Achievement" highest honor (1977). First star to challenge Hollywood studio system in court, she refuses to play poorly written roles, goes on strike, and is suspended without pay. While she loses the legal battle, she ultimately gets the parts, scripts, and recognition. Ocars: *Dangerous* (1935); *Jezebel* (1938); ten nominations.

1951: First American Women in Radio and Television convention is held in New York City. 1992: "Barney," the purple dinosaur brainchild of Tex. teacher Sheryl Leach, debuts on PBS-TV.

1805: Sacagawea, Indian guide, 19, with two-month-old son on her back, leads Lewis and Clark to the Pacific coast. 1944: Julia Phillips, b. New York City. First woman producer to win Oscar, *The Sting* (1974). 1987: Opening of National Museum of Women in the Arts in Washington, D.C., founded by Wilhelmina Cole Holladay, the first to be devoted to women artists. 1993: Marjorie Scardino, 46, is first woman and first American CEO of 150-year-old London-based *Economist* magazine.

1893: Mary Pickford, b. Toronto, Canada. "America's Sweetheart" is the first woman to form her own film company, 1916; cofounder, United Artists (1919). 1909: Women in Communications journalism society is founded by seven students at Univ. of Wash. in Seattle. 1918: Betty Bloomer Ford, b. Chicago. First Lady, 1974–1977. She focuses public attention on mammogram tests following her mastectomy (1974). Cofounder, Betty Ford Drug Treatment Center (1982). 1938: Eleanor Holmes Norton, b. Washington, D.C. First woman chair, New York City Commission on Human Rights (1970). Elected D.C. congressional representative, 1990 to present.

Mary Pickford

1939: Marian Anderson sings Easter Sunday concert for more than seventy-five thousand at Lincoln Memorial in Washington. In 1939 the Daughters of the American Revolution refused to let her use Constitution Hall; First Lady Eleanor Roosevelt resigned from the DAR in protest, which led to this historic concert. 1991: A record number—eleven— of Pulitzer Prizes are awarded to women.

1880: Frances Perkins, b. Boston. First woman U.S. cabinet member, as secretary of labor, 1933–1945. Defends decision to retain maiden name in court (1913). 1903: Clare Boothe Luce, b. New York City. Playright, *The Women* (1946). Two-term U.S. congresswoman, a Republican from Conn., beginning 1943. Delivers keynote address, Republican National Convention (1944). Ambassador to Italy, 1953–1956; to Brazil, 1959. "No good deed goes unpunished." 1930: Dolores Huerta, b. Dawson, N.M. Cofounder, VP, United Farm Workers Union. 1987: Katherine Fanning is first woman president, American Society of Newspaper Editors; editor, *Christian Science Monitor*, 1983 to present.

1912: Elinor Guggenheimer, b. New York City. Founding president, U.S. Women's Forum, 1973; International, 1983 to present. Cofounder in 1972 of the National Women's Political Caucus. 1941: Ellen Goodman, b. Newton, Mass. Syndicated columnist, 1976 to present; Pulitzer Prize for Commentary (1980). 1945: Kay Koplovitz, b. Milwaukee, Wis. President, CEO, USA Cable Network, 1980 to present. Cofounder, Women in Cable. 1980: Equal Opportunity Commission issues regulations prohibiting sexual harassment of women by superiors in government or business.

12 1917: Marietta Peabody Tree, b. Lawrence, Mass. First woman ambassador to UN (1964); first woman chief U.S. delegate to UN (1961). 1991: Yale's Skull and Bones undergraduate members vote to admit women.

13 1886: Ethel Leginska, b. England. Pioneer woman symphonic conductor. Founder, Boston Philharmonic (1926). 1909: Eudora Welty, b. Jackson, Miss. Pulitzer Prize, *The Optimist's Daughter* (1972). 1979: U.S. National Weather Service begins alternating names of storms for men and women.

14 1977: Congressional Caucus for Women's Issues is established by the eighteen women in the House, led by Rep. Margaret Heckler. In 1981 they will introduce the Women's Economic Equity Act, a package of bills on survival issues including pensions, child care, and insurance.

15 1865: Emily Smith Putnam, b. Canandaigua, N.Y. In 1900, as Barnard College president, she informs trustees she is pregnant, and they request her resignation. 1928: Norma Merrick Sklarek, b. New York City. First African-American woman licensed architect in U.S.: N.Y. and Calif. Designs Los Angeles Airport Terminal One. 1951: Heloise (Cruse Evans), b. Waco, Tex. Inherits mother's "Hints from Heloise" column. 1959: Emma Thompson, b. London. Oscar, *Howard's End* (1992). Cowriter, coproducer, codirector Cambridge Univ. first all-female review (1983).

1912: Harriett Quimby is first woman pilot to fly across English Channel. She dies in crash three months later. "Ambitious to be among the pathfinders, she took her chances like a man and died like one."

1885: Isak Dinesen (pseudonym of Karen Blixen), b. Denmark. Her autobiography, *Out of Africa*, is made into film and receives an Oscar (1985). "The cure for anything is salt water—sweat, tears, or the sea." 1916: Sirimavo Bandaranaike, b. Ceylon, now Sri Lanka. Becomes world's first woman prime minister when her husband is assassinated and she succeeds him, 1960–1965; 1970–1977.

1979: Los Angeles court awards "palimony" as compensation for ending a relationship.

1935: Loretta Lynn, b. Butcher's Hollow, Ky. First woman to win Country Music Assn.'s "Entertainer of the Year" award (1972). Elected to Country Music Hall of Fame (1988). 1949: Paloma Picasso, b. Paris. Fashion, jewelry designer. 1967: "K. Switzer," 20, disguised as a man, crosses finish line in Boston Marathon. She will be woman winner in 1974 New York Marathon. Women officially start to compete in Boston in 1972. Almost 2,000 women enter the 1993 Boston Marathon.

1939: *Glamour* magazine, "for the girl with the job," debuts with "Dos and Don'ts" column. Ruth Whitney is named editor in chief, 1967 to present.

1816: Charlotte Brontë, b. Yorkshire, England. She sends her poetry to England's poet laureate Robert Southey, who responds, "Literature cannot be the business of a woman's life." Using pseudonym "Currer Bell," she publishes *Jane Eyre* (1847). 1926: Queen Elizabeth II, England, b. London. In June the Trooping of the Colours marks queen's official birthday celebration.

1451: Isabella I, Queen of Spain, b. Spain. Finances Columbus's voyage in 1492.

1928: Shirley Temple Black, b. Santa Monica, Calif. Top Hollywood box office star, 1935–1938; retires at 22. U.S. delegate, UN; ambassador to Ghana, 1974–1976; to Czechoslovakia, 1989–1992; in 1976 first woman chief of protocol, State Dept. **1947:** Bernadette Devlin McAliskey, b. Northern Ireland. Youngest woman elected to British Parliament at 21, 1968.

1934: Shirley MacLaine, b. Richmond, Va. Actress, author. **1942:** Barbra Streisand, b. Brooklyn. Top-selling woman recording artist of all time. Signs $60 million record contract in 1993. Recipient of Oscar, Emmy, Tony, and Grammy.

1918: Ella Fitzgerald, b. Newport News, Va. "First Lady of Song." Jazz singer is discovered in amateur contest at the Apollo Theater, in New York City, in 1934. Inducted into Apollo Hall of Fame in 1993.

1777: Sybil Ludington, 16, rides from town to town, warning that the Redcoats are coming, and rallies volunteers to repel British the next day. She covers double the distance of Paul Revere. 1895: Dorothea Lange, b. Hoboken, N.J. Documentary photographer. 1923: Queen Mother, Lady Elizabeth Bowes-Lyon, marries duke of York, who will become King George VI. Daughter Elizabeth will become queen. 1936: Carol Burnett, b. San Antonio, Tex. Actress, comedienne. 1944: Cathleen Black, b. Chicago. First woman publisher of a weekly magazine, *New York* (1979); first woman publisher, *USA Today* (1983). First woman CEO and president, Newspaper Assn. of America (1992).

1759: Mary Wollstonecraft Godwin, b. London. Author, *The Vindication of the Rights of Women* (1792); demands equal rights in education. 1927: Coretta Scott King, b. Marion, Ala. Widow of Martin Luther King at 41 in 1968. President, CEO, King Center for Non-Violent Social Change; chair, King Federal Holiday Commission (1984). 1992: Betty Boothroyud becomes the first woman Speaker of British House of Commons in six centuries.

1993: More than one million girls age 9 to 15 participate in the first "Take Our Daughters to Work" day, sponsored by the Ms. Foundation for Women. This event was brought about because research showed that girls suffer a severe loss of self-esteem as they move through their teens. 1993: Pentagon orders military to drop most of its restrictions on women in aerial and naval combat.

1926: Rep. Carrie Meek, b. Tallahassee, Fla. This 68-year-old grandmother, the twelfth child of sharecroppers and grand-daughter of slaves, becomes in 1993 the first African-American woman in 129 years to represent Fla. in Congress. 1958: Michelle Pfeiffer, b. Santa Ana, Calif. Actress.

1939: Ellen Zwillich, b. Miami, Fla. First woman Pulitzer Prize for Music (1983); first woman Ph.D. in composition, Juilliard (1975). 1972: *The New York Times* eliminates separate male and female Help Wanted classified ads. The Supreme Court outlaws sex-segregated ads in 1973.

Coretta Scott King

MAY

1864: Anna M. Jarvis, b. Grafton, W.Va. In 1908 originates Mother's Day on anniversary of her mother's death. In 1914 Pres. Woodrow Wilson proclaims second Sunday in May as Mother's Day. 1940: Elsa Peretti, b. Florence, Italy. One of the first women to design jewelry and decorative objects exclusively for Tiffany & Co. (1974 to present). 1970: *Essence* magazine debuts.

1901: Doris Fleeson, b. Sterling, Kans. First syndicated woman political writer, 1946–1970, appearing in one hundred newspapers. 1991: *La Mujer Obrera* (The Working Woman) strike: Hispanic garment workers with ILGWU strike to improve working conditions.

1974: The Women's Sports Foundation is founded by Billie Jean King. 1984: Dr. Luella Klein becomes the first and only woman president of the American College of Obstetricians and Gynecologists, founded in 1951. By 1993, women compose 25% of ACOG membership and 55% of first-year ob/gyn residents.

1855: St. Luke's Hospital in New York City opens. It is the first hospital to treat women's diseases and the "birthplace of gynecology." 1929: Audrey Hepburn, b. Brussels. Oscar-winning actress; special ambassador for UNICEF. 1931: Paige Rense, b. Des Moines. Editor, *Architectural Digest*, 1970 to present. 1979: Margaret Thatcher, 53, Oxford graduate, becomes Britain's first woman prime minister and its longest serving in the twentieth century, twelve years; resigns in 1990. "Any woman who understands the problems of running a home will be nearer to understanding the problems of running a country." 1987: Supreme Court rules women must be admitted to the Rotary Club.

Billie Jean King

1921: Coco Chanel introduces Chanel No. 5 perfume on the fifth day of the fifth month. 1942: Tammy Wynette, b. Tupelo, Miss. "First Lady of Country Music." "Stand By Your Man" is biggest-selling country single in history.

1885: *Good Housekeeping*, the first magazine for women, debuts as a biweekly to "produce and perpetuate perfection—or as near unto perfection—as may be attained in the household."

1912: Forty women establish Advertising Women of N.Y., after being denied admittance to men's club. 1919: Eva Perón, b. Argentina. Cogoverns with husband, Juan Perón, from 1946 until 1952, the time of her death. 1926: Voting age for British women is lowered to 21 from 30. 1927: Ruth Prawer Jhabvala, b. Cologne, Germany. Screenwriter. Oscars: *A Room with a View* (1986); *Howard's End* (1992); *Remains of the Day* (1993).

1874: Mass. legislature passes the first ten-hour-a-day work limit for women and minors. 1952: Beth Henley, b. Jackson, Miss. Dramatist. Pulitzer Prize, *Crimes of the Heart* (1981).

1936: Glenda Jackson, b. Cheshire, England. Oscars: *Women in Love* (1970); *A Touch of Class* (1973). Elected to British Parliament (1992). 1946: Candice Bergen, b. Beverly Hills, Calif. Actress. "Murphy Brown," 1988 to present. 1960: FDA approves birth-control pill.

1872: Victoria Woodhull is nominated as the first woman candidate for U.S. president. 1898: Ariel Durant, b. Russia. Coauthor, with husband, Will, eleven-volume *History of Civilization*; wins 1926 Pulitzer Prize. 1900: Cecilia Payne-Gaposhkin, b. England. First woman tenured professor, Harvard (1956). From 1956 to 1960 serves as first woman chair, astronomy dept. 1919: Ella Grasso, b. Windsor Locks, Conn. First woman elected governor in her own right in the state of Conn. (1975–1980). 1934: Judith Jamison, b. Philadelphia. Dancer, director.

1894: Martha Graham, b. Pittsburgh, Pa. Doyenne of modern dance; forms own company in 1926. Premieres 180th ballet at 96; performs until she is 75. Pres. Ford awards her Medal of Freedom. 1956: Financial Women's Assn. is founded by eight women on Wall Street for senior executives who are excluded from male business clubs.

Martha Graham

1820: Florence Nightingale, b. Florence. "The Lady with the Lamp" is mother of modern nursing. English people raise forty-four thousand pounds to fund Nightingale School of Nursing. Queen Victoria honors her as the first woman awarded Order of Merit. 1985: Amy Eilberg, 30, is ordained the first woman Conservative rabbi, Jewish Theological Seminary, New York City.

1907: Daphne Du Maurier, b. London. Author, classic Gothic novels, *Rebecca* (1938). 1937: Judith Somogi, b. New York City. First woman to conduct an opera in U.S.; music director, conductor, Utica (N.Y.) Symphony, 1977–1988.

Florence Nightingale

1971: Senate appoints the first female pages; House follows in 1973. 1973: Supreme Court rules that women in armed forces are entitled to the same spouses' benefits as those for male servicemen.

1930: Ellen Church becomes the first air stewardess at a time when an applicant had to be a registered nurse, 25 or younger, weigh under 115 pounds, and not exceed five four. In the seventies, airlines recruit male and female flight attendants. By 1993, age, marital, and pregnancy restrictions no longer apply. 1937: Madeline Albright, b. Prague. U.S. ambassador to UN, cabinet position, 1993 to present.

1881: Anne O'Hare McCormick, b. Yorkshire, England. First woman on the editorial board, *The New York Times* (1936); first woman to win Pulitzer Prize for Foreign Correspondence (1937). 1929: Adrienne Rich, b. Baltimore. When the future poet attends Radcliffe, only men teach and only male poets are studied. She accepts her 1974 National Book Award on behalf of all women. 1975: Junko Tabei, deputy leader of the Japanese all-woman expedition, becomes the first woman to reach the summit of Mt. Everest. "Thank goodness I don't have to go any higher." 1991: Edith Cresson, 57, becomes the first woman premier of France.

1879: Lady Nancy Astor, b. Danville, Va. First woman member of British Parliament, 1919–1945. She notes, "I married beneath me—all women do." In 1920 first woman to speak in House of Commons. Advocates women's rights, child welfare. 1978: Women join White House Honor Guard, a move initiated by Rosalynn Carter.

1979: Executive Order on Women's Business Enterprise directs federal agencies to establish goals for contract awards to businesses owned by women. The Office of Women's Business Ownership is established by Small Business Administration (SBA). 1992: Lady Jean Denton is appointed by the prime minister as cochair of the Women's National Commission, to ensure that women's views are considered in government policy-making. Two-time British Woman Racing Driver champion. President, U.K. Women's Forum.

1930: Lorraine Hansberry, b. Chicago. The first African-American woman to produce a play on Broadway; her autobiographical *A Raisin in the Sun* opens in 1959. In this N.Y. Drama Critics award-winning play, she warns that a "dream deferred" will "dry up/like a raisin in the sun," or it will explode. She dies of cancer at 34. 1941: Nora Ephron, b. New York City. Screenwriter, *Heartburn* (1983); *Silkwood* (1983); *When Harry Met Sally* (1989); director, *Sleepless in Seattle* (1993). 1941: Jane Brody, b. Brooklyn. Syndicated *New York Times* nutrition columnist. 1947: Glenn Close, b. Greenwich, Conn. Tonys: "The Real Thing" (1984); "Death and the Maiden" (1992).

1768: Dolley Madison, b. N.C. First Lady, 1809–1817. As British troops burn Washington, she flees with Gilbert Stuart's portrait of George Washington and state documents. 1901: Doris Fleeson, b. Sterling, Kans. First syndicated woman political columnist (1945). Cofounder, American Newspaper Guild.

1909: Sister Maria Innocentia Hummel, b. Bavaria. Beginning in 1935, art teacher's drawings are created into M. I. Hummel figurines. 1912: Mary McCarthy, b. Seattle. Author, critic. 1973: Lynn Genesko, a swimmer, receives from the Univ. of Miami the first athletic scholarship to a woman. 1980: May 21 and 28, the first women graduate from U.S. service academies.

1844: Mary (Stevenson) Cassatt, b. Pittsburgh, Pa. Impressionist painter; noted for depictions of mothers and children.
1849: Bertha Honore Palmer, b. Louisville, Ky. Organizes "Woman's Building" at Chicago's World Exhibition of 1893,
featuring achievements of women from forty-seven nations. 1993: Patricia Cloherty is first woman to head major venture
capital firm (funded Apple Computer). In 1994 she is the first woman president, National Venture Capital Assn. Founding
president, Committee of 200.

Mary Cassatt

1810: Margaret Fuller, b. Cambridge, Mass. First woman journalist in U.S., at *New York Tribune*. First woman foreign correspondent (1846). 1990: Mills College students end their successful two-week strike to keep the college only for women when the Mills Board of Trustees reverses its decision to admit undergraduate men. Founded in 1852 and located in Oakland, Calif., Mills is the oldest women's college west of the Rockies.

1878: Lillian Gilbreth, b. Oakland, Calif. Industrial engineer and mother of twelve innovates foot-pedal trash cans and storage shelves on refrigerator doors. 1898: Helen Brooke Taussig, b. Cambridge, Mass. First woman president, American Heart Assn. (1965). Pioneers "blue baby" surgery to correct congenital defects (1944). 1905: Claire McCardell, b. Frederick, Md. Fashion designer creates "separates," stretch leotard bodysuit, moderate-price ready-to-wear; popularizes denim.

1929: Beverly Sills, b. Brooklyn. Operatic soprano joins New York City Opera in 1955; becomes director when she retires twenty-five years later; holds position from 1979 to 1989. First woman elected chair, Lincoln Center for the Performing Arts, New York City (1994). 1931: The Academy of Motion Picture Arts and Sciences names its award trophy "Oscar" after Mrs. Herrick, academy secretary, says the figurine "looks like my uncle Oscar."

1909: Eugenie Moore Andersen, b. Adair, Iowa. Serving in Denmark from 1949 to 1953, she is first U. S. woman ambassador to that country. 1952: Marion Bacon, of the Vassar Cooperative Bookshop in Poughkeepsie, N.Y., is named first woman president of American Booksellers Assn. 1992: Vicki Randle, percussionist, becomes the first woman in the "Tonight" show band.

1818: Amelia Jenks Bloomer, b. Homer, N.Y. Publishes first newspaper for women, the *Lily* (1849). Women's rights activist promotes sensible dress—bloomers—invented by her cousin Elizabeth Miller. In 1850s skirts reaching only four inches below the knee are considered scandalous. "In the minds of some people the short dress and women's rights were inseparably connected." In the mid-70s pantsuits are barred from public restaurants. 1819: Julia Ward Howe, b. New York City. Her "Battle Hymn of the Republic" (1862) becomes Union Army theme. 1907: Rachel Carson, b. Springdale, Pa. *The Silent Spring* (1962) warns of dangerous pesticides to ecology.

Janet Guthrie

1858: Lizzie Black Kander, b. Milwaukee, Wis. Author, *The Settlement Cook Book: The Way to a Man's Heart*. By late 1970s, more than one million copies will be sold.

1895: Jane Grant, b. Joplin, Mo. First woman to cover a city-room desk, at *The New York Times* (1914–1930). She specialized in women's news and covered the rise of the suffrage movement until it became front-page news and then male reporters were assigned. Cofounder, *The New Yorker* (1925). 1977: "In company with the first lady ever to qualify at Indianapolis, gentlemen, start your engines." Champion race car driver Janet Guthrie, 39, becomes first woman to complete Indy 500.

1886: Dorothy Eustis, b. Philadelphia. Founder, the "Seeing Eye" guide dog training school (1930). **1946:** Candy Lightner, b. Dallas, Tex. Founder, in 1979, of Mothers Against Drunk Driving (MADD), in memory of 13-year-old daughter.

1924: Patricia Roberts Harris, b. Mattoon, Ill. First woman to hold two U.S. cabinet positions: secretary of HUD from 1977 to 1979 and secretary of HEW from 1979 to 1981. First African-American woman dean of a law school, Howard Univ. (1969). **1982:** Ellen Burstyn becomes first woman president of Actor's Equity, founded in 1913. Oscar, *Alice Doesn't Live Here Anymore* (1974).

JUNE

1910: Mrs. John Bruce Dodd launches Father's Day to honor her widowed father. The first Father's Day is observed in Spokane, Wash., on the third Sunday in June. 1895: Hattie McDaniel, b. Wichita, Kans. First African-American Oscar winner, for role of Mammy in *Gone With the Wind* (1940). 1926: Marilyn Monroe, b. Los Angeles. Her twenty-three movies gross more than $200 million in first runs. 1993: Connie Chung, 46, becomes the second woman co-anchor of evening news, CBS, seventeen years after Barbara Walters became the first, for ABC in 1976.

1953: Queen Elizabeth II's coronation.

1906: Josephine Baker, b. St. Louis. First African-American woman to become an international star. Jazz entertainer fights for desegregated theaters and restaurants in the fifties and refuses to play in segregated clubs. 1924: Colleen Dewhurst, b. Montreal, Canada. President, Actors Equity (1985). 1970: *Washington Post* staff memo urges reporters to use gender-sensitive language when writing about women. 1972: Sally J. Priesand, 25, is ordained the first woman rabbi in Reform Judaism. Little more than a decade later women rabbis are accepted in Conservative Judaism.

1928: "Dr. Ruth" Westheimer, b. Germany. Pioneer media sex therapist. 1940: Lynne "Angel" and Paul Harvey wed. She is executive producer of his number-one network radio shows starting in the forties and runs their production company.

Josephine Baker

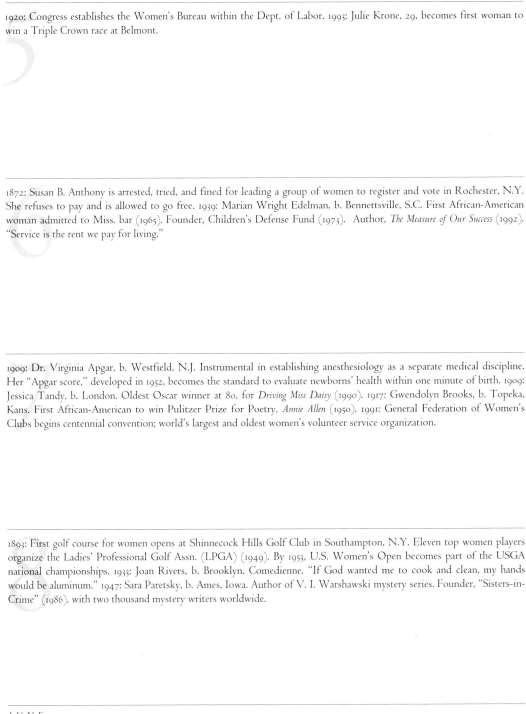

1920: Congress establishes the Women's Bureau within the Dept. of Labor. 1993: Julie Krone, 29, becomes first woman to win a Triple Crown race at Belmont.

1872: Susan B. Anthony is arrested, tried, and fined for leading a group of women to register and vote in Rochester, N.Y. She refuses to pay and is allowed to go free. 1939: Marian Wright Edelman, b. Bennettsville, S.C. First African-American woman admitted to Miss. bar (1965). Founder, Children's Defense Fund (1973). Author, *The Measure of Our Success* (1992). "Service is the rent we pay for living."

1909: Dr. Virginia Apgar, b. Westfield, N.J. Instrumental in establishing anesthesiology as a separate medical discipline. Her "Apgar score," developed in 1952, becomes the standard to evaluate newborns' health within one minute of birth. 1909: Jessica Tandy, b. London. Oldest Oscar winner at 80, for *Driving Miss Daisy* (1990). 1917: Gwendolyn Brooks, b. Topeka, Kans. First African-American to win Pulitzer Prize for Poetry, *Annie Allen* (1950). 1991: General Federation of Women's Clubs begins centennial convention; world's largest and oldest women's volunteer service organization.

1893: First golf course for women opens at Shinnecock Hills Golf Club in Southampton, N.Y. Eleven top women players organize the Ladies' Professional Golf Assn. (LPGA) (1949). By 1953, U.S. Women's Open becomes part of the USGA national championships. 1933: Joan Rivers, b. Brooklyn. Comedienne. "If God wanted me to cook and clean, my hands would be aluminum." 1947: Sara Paretsky, b. Ames, Iowa. Author of V. I. Warshawski mystery series. Founder, "Sisters-in-Crime" (1986), with two thousand mystery writers worldwide.

1836: Elizabeth Garrett Anderson, b. England. First British woman M.D. 1843: Baroness Bertha Kinsky von Suttner, b. Prague. In 1905 first woman to win Nobel Peace Prize, *Lay Down Your Arms* (1889). 1887: Gertrude Muller, b. Leo, Ind. Inventor and manufacturer of safe juvenile products: portable "toidey seat" (1924); child auto seat.

1922: Judy Garland, b. Grand Rapids, Minn. Singer, actress. Played Dorothy in *The Wizard of Oz* (1939). 1930: Grace Mirabella, b. Maplewood, N.J. *Vogue* editor from 1952 to 1988. In June 1989, her namesake magazine, *Mirabella*, debuts. 1981: Supreme Court rules on wage discrimination that women may sue for equal pay, even if their work is not identical with that of male employees.

1769: Anne Newport Royall, b. Baltimore. Upon becoming a widow at 54, she becomes the first American newspaper-woman. First woman journalist to get exclusive interview with a president, John Quincy Adams. In 1830 she publishes weekly gossip newspaper in Washington, D.C.

1930: Anne Frank, b. Frankfurt, Germany. On her thirteenth birthday she receives a diary. *The Diary of a Young Girl* (1952) is written during her two years of hiding from the Nazis. She dies at 15 in a German concentration camp. In 1947, her father, the only family survivor, publishes her diary. 1974: Little League abolishes boys-only policy following sex-discrimination suits in fifteen states.

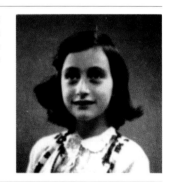

Anne Frank

1934: Marianne Means, b. Sioux City, Iowa. First woman reporter assigned to cover White House full-time; from 1961 to 1965 she reports for the Hearst newspapers. 1993: Tansu Ciller, 47, becomes first woman prime minister of Turkey. Third woman to head Muslim country, following Benazir Bhutto, Pakistan, and Begum Khalida Zia, Bangladesh.

1811: Harriet Beecher Stowe, b. Litchfield, Conn. When the author of *Uncle Tom's Cabin* meets Pres. Lincoln, he says, "So you're the little woman who wrote the book that made this great war." In one week in 1852, ten thousand copies are sold; by late 1853, more than three hundred thousand. 1904: Margaret Bourke-White, b. New York City. Photo essayist; first woman war correspondent to U.S. Army (1942). *Life* editor from 1936 to 1969. 1969: Steffi Graf, b. Germany. Wins fourteen tennis grand slams (1987–1993).

1887: Malvina Hoffman, b. New York City. Sculptor taught by Rodin creates 110 life-size figures for Field Museum, Chicago (1933). 1869: Arabella Bobb Mansfield, 23, is the first woman admitted to the bar in the U.S., in Iowa. (Margaret Brent was the first woman lawyer in the U.S., in 1648, in Baltimore.) In 1918 the American Bar Assn. accepts its first woman member; by 1992 women compose 25% of membership. Roberta Cooper Ramo becomes the first woman president of the ABA in 1995. 1988: Census Bureau reports that in 1987, 51% of all new mothers remain in the job market.

1917: Katharine Meyer Graham, b. New York City. Publisher, chair, CEO, Washington Post Co., *Newsweek* (1969–1993); Pulitzer Prize, Watergate story. First woman on Associated Press board (1974). First woman CEO of *Fortune* 500 company. 1993: Wellesley College receives almost $11 million, the most donations from alumni, on per student basis, of all U.S. colleges.

Katharine Meyer Graham

1963: Soviet cosmonaut Valentina Tereshkova, 26, becomes the first woman in space. 1970: McSorley's century-old men-only saloon in New York City is ordered by federal court to admit women. Mory's, Yale's famous all-male bar, will open to women after suit in 1974.

1983: Dr. Sally Ride, 32, becomes the first American woman in space on *Challenger* mission.

1896: Wallis Warfield, b. Pa. Edward VIII abdicates British throne to marry her. On Dec. 12, 1936, he explains in radio broadcast, "I have found it impossible to carry on the heavy burden of responsibility . . . without the help and support of the woman I love." They marry June 3, 1937, in France, and she becomes Duchess of Windsor. 1986: Supreme Court rules sexual harassment is discrimination. 1986: Beginning today, *The New York Times* will use "Ms." as an honorific in its news columns. The *Times* now believes "Ms." has become a part of the language.

1905: Lillian Hellman, b. New Orleans. Dramatist, author. During McCarthy hearings in 1952, she tells House Un-American Activities Committee, "I cannot and will not cut my conscience to fit this year's fashion," and is not forced to testify. 1948: Frieda Barkin Hennock is first woman Federal Communications Commission (FCC) commissioner; advocates reserving channels for educational TV and controls for children's programming. 1988: Supreme Court unanimously upholds law enforcing admission of women to private clubs.

1908: More than twenty thousand suffragettes demonstrate in London.

21

1907: Anne Morrow Lindbergh, b. Englewood, N.J. In *Gift from the Sea* (1955), she writes, "By and large, mothers and house-wives are the only workers who do not have regular time off. They are the great vacationless class." 1909: Katherine Dunham, b. Joliet, Ill. "Grande dame of American dance" organizes first professional African-American dance troupe (1930s). 1933: Sen. Dianne Feinstein, b. San Francisco. Former San Francisco mayor is elected in 1992, along with Barbara Boxer; first time a state elects two woman senators. 1993: Karen Nussbaum becomes director, Women's Bureau, Dept. of Labor. Founder, "9 to 5," the National Assn. of Working Women (1973); inspired film. 1993: Hannah Troy, who invented the petite size, dies. She studied military measurements of WWII women volunteers and the statistics confirmed that the typical U.S. woman is short-waisted.

Anne Morrow Lindbergh and Charles Lindbergh

1940: Wilma Rudolph, b. St. Bethlehem, Tenn. "La Gazelle" is first American woman runner to win three gold medals at single Olympics (1960). Olympic Hall of Fame (1983). First woman honoree, National Sports Awards (1993). 1949: First twelve women graduate from Harvard Medical School, founded in 1783. Women will compose 49.5% of the class of 1997.

1916: Mary Pickford, who began as a $5-a-day extra in 1909, signs the first million-dollar movie contract, months before Charlie Chaplin. 1976: A Md. Court of Appeals rules that a person's housework has monetary value. 1991: Dr. Bernadine P. Healy, 47, a cardiologist, becomes the first woman director of the National Institutes of Health (NIH). She launches ten-year, $500 million Women's Health Initiative, which focuses on the ailments of older women.

1903: Mme. Marie Curie announces discovery of radium. She shares Nobel Prize with husband, Pierre. After his death, she isolates radium in its pure state and receives second Nobel Prize. In 1934 she will die of radiation exposure. 1993: Kim Campbell, 46, is sworn in as Canada's first woman prime minister.

1812: Fanny Palmer, b. Leicester, England. First recognized woman lithographer, Currier & Ives (1849–1868). 1892: Pearl S. Buck, b. Hillsboro, W.Va. Only woman to receive both the Pulitzer Prize for *The Good Earth* (1932) and the Nobel Prize for Literature for the body of her work (1938). 1902: Antonia Brico, b. Netherlands. First woman conductor, N.Y. Philharmonic (1939). 1913: Emily Dawson becomes first woman magistrate in London. 1914: Babe Didrickson Zaharias, b. Tex. Called the "greatest" woman athlete. Pro golfer; cofounder, LPGA (1949). Olympic track medalist, two gold, one silver.

Marie Curie

Helen Keller

1859: Mildred J. Hill, b. Louisville, Ky. Composer, "Happy Birthday," the world's most popular song; sister Patty Smith Hill wrote the lyrics. To own exclusive rights to the song from 1988 to 2010, Warner Communications pays $25 million. 1880: Helen Keller, b. Tuscumbia, Ala. Becomes blind, deaf, and mute at 19 months from scarlet fever. Taught by Anne Sullivan, she graduates from Radcliffe with distinction (1904).

1876: Clara Maas, b. E. Orange, N.J. Army nurse is the only woman and American to die of yellow fever, after volunteering for Maj. Walter Reed's immunization experiment, on Aug. 24, 1901. 1888: Antoinette Perry, b. Denver, Colo. Cofounder, American Theater Wing. Annual Antoinette Perry Award, "Tony," honors theatrical achievements (1947 to present). 1990: Smithsonian Institution opens "From Parlor to Politics," a permanent exhibit to recognize women's contributions.

1885: Virginia Pope, b. Chicago. Dean of fashion editors; *The New York Times* (1933–1955). Positions American designers as a world influence. Cofounder, Fashion Institute of Technology. 1887: Elizabeth Cotten, b. Chapel Hill, N.C. She will die at 95 on this day. At 11, the folk guitarist composed the classic "Freight Train," to which she finally secured copyright when she was 65. Developed "Cotten picking" guitar style.

1917: Lena Horne, b. Brooklyn. Singer, actress. First African-American woman to sign long-term Hollywood contract. In 1940s and 1950s, she fights for contracts guaranteeing that African-Americans can attend her shows. 1940: "Brenda Starr, Reporter" debuts in *Chicago Tribune*. Creator Dale Messick, 34, changes her name from Dalia and submits cartoons by mail. "Wonder Woman" debuts in 1940 as female crusader for justice, with superhuman ability to deflect bullets with her Amazonium bracelets. 1982: On March 22, 1972, the senate passed the Equal Rights Amendment prohibiting sexual discrimination. It was then sent to the states for ratification and despite the 1978 extension was only ratified by thirty-five of the required thirty-eight states, and failed to pass.

JULY

1908: Estee Lauder, b. Queens, N.Y. Cosmetics tycoon starts worldwide empire with her uncle's face cream in 1946. In 1993, she is the only woman on *Forbes* 400 list (minimum worth $300 million) to have made it on her own. **1961:** Princess Diana, b. Sandringham, England. On July 29, 1981, at 20 years of age, she marries Prince Charles. **1984:** Male voters in Liechtenstein give women the right to vote. **1993:** Carol Bellamy becomes head of Peace Corps. **1994:** Dr. Rosann Spiro is first woman chair of American Marketing Assn., founded 1937.

1939: Judy Chicago, b. Chicago. Artist's *The Dinner Party* depicts women's social history. **1993:** Dr. Sheila E. Widnall, 54, an aeronautical engineer, is secretary of the air force; first woman in charge of a military service. First woman faculty chair, MIT.

1796: Maria Martin, b. Charleston, S.C. Audubon's only woman assistant; paints backgrounds for watercolor bird portraits. **1990:** N.J. Supreme Court orders Princeton's remaining men-only clubs to admit women.

1777: Mary Katherine Goddard publishes the Declaration of Independence in Baltimore, where she is the only printer. She continues to publish Baltimore's only newspaper during the Revolution. Benjamin Franklin appoints her the first woman to hold a federal position, as Baltimore's postmaster (1775–1789). **1918:** Twins Esther Pauline Friedman ("Dear Ann Landers," Oct. 1955 to the present) and Pauline Esther Friedman ("Dear Abby" Abigail Van Buren, Jan. 1956 to the present) b. Sioux City, Iowa. **1987:** Lions Club International votes to admit women.

Independence Day

Ann Landers

1989: Jean Briggs is first woman assistant managing editor, *Forbes*. Ruth Gruenberg was first woman senior editor (1977).

1866: Beatrix Potter, b. London. Author, illustrator, *The Tale of Peter Rabbit*. 1993: Elizabeth Larson is the only woman on *Financial World*'s "Top 100 1992 Earners" list, ranks sixty-eighth: $8 million plus.

1861: Nettie Stevens, b. Cavendish, Vt. In 1903 biologist discovers that sex is determined by X (female) or Y (male) chromosome. 1887: Beatrice Fox Auerbach, b. Hartford, Conn. Pres., G. Fox & Co. department store in Hartford (1938–1965); largest privately owned department store in U.S. Pioneers five-day workweek, retirement plans, medical and lunch facilities, interest-free loans. Institutes free delivery service, toll-free telephone order department, automated billing. 1965: Pres. Lyndon B. Johnson creates cabinet-level Equal Opportunity Commission. 1987: Kiwanis International votes to admit women members.

1943: Faye Wattleton, b. St. Louis. Nurse becomes the first woman, first African-American, and youngest president of Planned Parenthood (1978–1992). 1951: Anjelica Huston, b. Los Angeles. Oscar, *Prizzi's Honor* (1985).

1893: Dorothy Thompson, b. Lancaster, N.Y. Central European bureau chief, Curtis newspapers (1924). In 1930s, she and Eleanor Roosevelt are considered the most influential women in America. 1901: Dame Barbara Cartland, b. England. Britain's "first lady of romance" is the world's best-selling and most prolific woman author, writing almost six hundred romance novels, averaging "one a fortnight since I was 70." 1926: Dr. Mathilde Krim, b. Italy. Geneticist founds and leads American Foundation for AIDS Research (AmFAR), 1983 to the present.

1875: Mary McLeod Bethune, b. Mayesville, S.C., the fifteenth of seventeen children, to slaves. Founder and president, National Council of Negro Women (1935). First African-American woman presidential adviser, to Franklin Delano Roosevelt and Harry Truman. Founder, Bethune-Cookman College.

1853: U.S. Commissioner of Patents employs the first women government workers, as clerks, despite objections to this innovation. Clara Barton is among the first women hired. 1971: The National Women's Political Caucus is organized by 321 women in Washington, D.C.

1976: Barbara Jordan becomes first African-American and first woman to make keynote speech at Democratic National Convention.

1910: *Women's Wear Daily* premieres as fashion industry trade newspaper; *W* debuts April 1972 as consumer lifestyle magazine.

1858: Emmeline Pankhurst, b. Manchester, England. Suffragette endures imprisonment to give British women the right to vote. In 1903, with daughter, Christable, organizes the Women's Social and Political Union with theme "Votes for Women." 1923: Frances Lear, b. Hudson, N.Y. Founder, publisher, *Lear's* (March 1988). 1972: Frances Westwood becomes first woman chair, Democratic National Committee.

Bastille Day

Emmeline Pankhurst (*third from left*)

1867: Maggie L. Walker, b. Richmond, Va. First woman bank president in U.S. at St. Luke Penny Saving Bank, in Richmond, 1903. When white bankers fail to lend money to keep the Richmond public schools open, her bank finances $100,000 loan. 1905: Dorothy Fields, b. Allenhurst, N.J. First woman to win Oscar for songwriting: "The Way You Look Tonight" (1937). First woman, Songwriters Hall of Fame (1971). More than four hundred songs include "On the Sunny Side of the Street," "I'm in the Mood for Love," "Lovely to Look At," and "Big Spender."

1821: Mary Baker Eddy, b. Concord, N.H. Founder, Christian Science movement (1876). At 87, founds the *Christian Science Monitor* (1908). 1862: Ida Wells-Barnett, b. Holly Springs, Miss. Cofounder, National Assn. for the Advancement of Colored People (NAACP). 1907: Barbara Stanwyck, b. Brooklyn. Actress is highest-paid woman in U.S. in 1944, earning $400,000 per year. 1911: Ginger Rogers, b. Independence, Mo. Fred Astaire's dance partner does everything Fred does, only she does it backward and in heels. 1947: Alexis Herman, b. Mobile, Ala. As special assistant to Pres. Bill Clinton for public liaison, she is the highest-ranking African-American to serve in the White House (1993 to the present).

Barbara Stanwyck

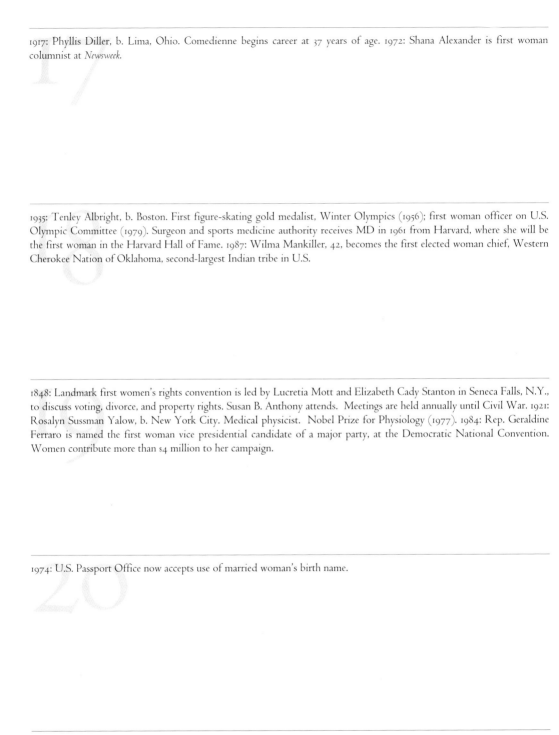

1917: Phyllis Diller, b. Lima, Ohio. Comedienne begins career at 37 years of age. 1972: Shana Alexander is first woman columnist at *Newsweek*.

1935: Tenley Albright, b. Boston. First figure-skating gold medalist, Winter Olympics (1956); first woman officer on U.S. Olympic Committee (1979). Surgeon and sports medicine authority receives MD in 1961 from Harvard, where she will be the first woman in the Harvard Hall of Fame. 1987: Wilma Mankiller, 42, becomes the first elected woman chief, Western Cherokee Nation of Oklahoma, second-largest Indian tribe in U.S.

1848: Landmark first women's rights convention is led by Lucretia Mott and Elizabeth Cady Stanton in Seneca Falls, N.Y., to discuss voting, divorce, and property rights. Susan B. Anthony attends. Meetings are held annually until Civil War. 1921: Rosalyn Sussman Yalow, b. New York City. Medical physicist. Nobel Prize for Physiology (1977). 1984: Rep. Geraldine Ferraro is named the first woman vice presidential candidate of a major party, at the Democratic National Convention. Women contribute more than $4 million to her campaign.

1974: U.S. Passport Office now accepts use of married woman's birth name.

1960: Sirimavo Bandaranaik becomes first woman prime minister in world; widow of murdered PM of Ceylon, now Sri Lanka.

1849: Emma Lazarus, b. New York City. Her sonnet is inscribed on base of Statue of Liberty (1883): "Give me your tired, your poor . . . your huddled masses yearning to breathe free. Send these, the homeless, tempest-tost to me. I lift my lamp beside the golden door!" 1939: Jane Mathilda Bolin becomes the first African-American woman U.S. judge, New York City Domestic Relations Court.

1972: Title IX of Education Amendments bans sex bias in federally funded programs. Within a decade, 500% more girls will compete in high school sports. 1985: Amy Shaughnessy becomes the first woman president of American Mensa, the international high IQ society (top 2% of population), founded in 1960. Women comprise 35% of the membership.

1897: Amelia Earhart, b. Atchison, Kans. First woman to cross the Atlantic solo in record time, May 20–21, 1932. On June 1, 1937 she takes off on round-the-world flight; last contact is July 2 as she disappears in South Pacific. 1920: Bella Abzug, b. New York City. First woman elected to Congress on a women's rights platform. First Jewish congresswoman (D-N.Y.), 1971–1977. Initiates the Congressional Caucus on Women's Issues. Presiding officer, International Woman's Year convention, Houston (1977); the first and only federally funded National Women's Conference.

25

1873: Anne Morgan, b. N.Y. Cofounder, Colony Club, N.Y.'s first social club for women (1903). 1874: Rose Cecil O'Neill, b. Wilkes-Barre, Pa. Illustrator creates Kewpie dolls, patented 1913.

26

1858: Ella Alexander Boole, b. Ohio. She runs unsuccessfully for Senate in 1920 with slogan "Send a mother to the Senate."; wins more than 150,000 votes. 1990: Congressional Caucus for Women's Issues introduces Women's Health Equity Act to address women's health problems, including $50 million for additional research.

Kewpie doll

1878: Genevieve Cline, b. Ohio. First woman federal judge (1928), U.S. Customs Court in New York City; serves twenty-five years. 1896: Helen Jarrell, b. Meriwether County, Ga. First woman superintendent of schools, Atlanta (1944).

1929: Jacqueline Bouvier Kennedy Onassis, b. Southampton, N.Y. Wife of President John F. Kennedy. First Lady at 31; (1961 to November 22, 1963). Establishes White House Historical Assn. Her restoration culminates in Emmy award-winning televised tour of the White House, viewed by 56 million Americans on February 14, 1962. To raise funds for the historic preservation, she creates a visitors tour book; $42 million profit will be collected by 1994. (She inspires National Endowment for the Arts.) Becomes a book editor after leaving the White House. Beginning in 1975, she leads rescue efforts for landmarks scheduled to be demolished in New York City, including Grand Central Station. At her death, she has the most listings of any living American woman in the *Reader's Guide to Periodical Literature*. Buried alongside her slain husband at Arlington National Cemetery.

1897: Dorothy Shaver, b. Center Point, Ark. As president of Lord & Taylor in 1945, her salary of $110,000 is highest on record for a woman in U.S. Champions American designers; creates first teenage department. Cofounder, The Fashion Group International; Costume Institute at Metropolitan Museum. 1930: Nancy Hays Teeter, b. Marion, Ind. First woman governor, Federal Reserve Bank (1978–1984). 1936: Elizabeth Hanford Dole, b. Salisbury, N.C. First woman secretary of transportation (1983–1987); secretary of labor (1989–1990); president, American Red Cross (1991 to the present).

1940: Patricia Schroeder, b. Portland, Oreg. First woman representative (Democrat) from Colo., now in her eleventh term (1993 to the present). Longest-sitting congresswoman is original sponsor of the Family & Medical Leave Act. Cochair with Rep. Olympia J. Snowe of Congressional Caucus for Women's Issues. 1956: Anita Hill, b. Okla., youngest of thirteen children. In October 1991 the law professor accuses now U.S. Supreme Court judge Clarence Thomas of sexual harassment in televised Senate confirmation hearings before all-male Judiciary Committee. 1992: Yael Arad, 25, wins Olympic silver medal in judo; first Israeli to win Olympic medal.

1944: Sherry Lansing, b. Chicago. First woman head of a Hollywood film studio, as president of production at Twentieth Century–Fox (1980–1982). Became chairwoman of Paramount Pictures in 1992.

31

AUGUST

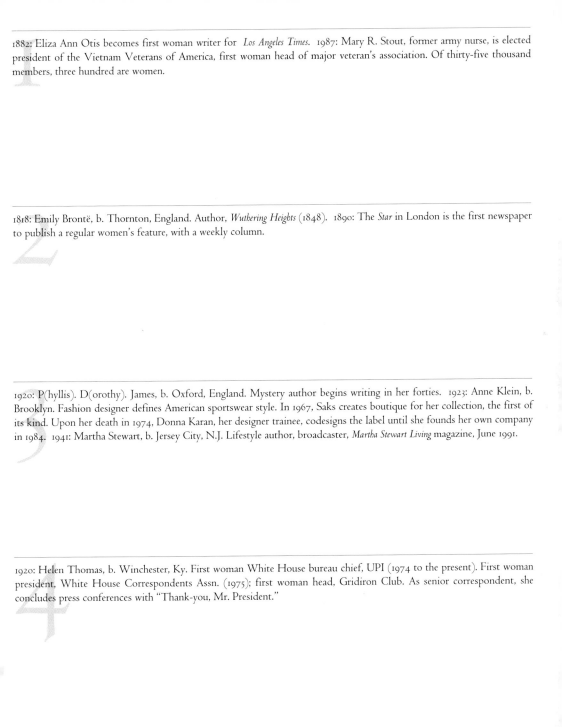

1 1882: Eliza Ann Otis becomes first woman writer for *Los Angeles Times*. 1987: Mary R. Stout, former army nurse, is elected president of the Vietnam Veterans of America, first woman head of major veteran's association. Of thirty-five thousand members, three hundred are women.

2 1818: Emily Brontë, b. Thornton, England. Author, *Wuthering Heights* (1848). 1890: The *Star* in London is the first newspaper to publish a regular women's feature, with a weekly column.

3 1920: P(hyllis). D(orothy). James, b. Oxford, England. Mystery author begins writing in her forties. 1923: Anne Klein, b. Brooklyn. Fashion designer defines American sportswear style. In 1967, Saks creates boutique for her collection, the first of its kind. Upon her death in 1974, Donna Karan, her designer trainee, codesigns the label until she founds her own company in 1984. 1941: Martha Stewart, b. Jersey City, N.J. Lifestyle author, broadcaster, *Martha Stewart Living* magazine, June 1991.

4 1920: Helen Thomas, b. Winchester, Ky. First woman White House bureau chief, UPI (1974 to the present). First woman president, White House Correspondents Assn. (1975); first woman head, Gridiron Club. As senior correspondent, she concludes press conferences with "Thank-you, Mr. President."

Anne Klein

Gertrude Ederle

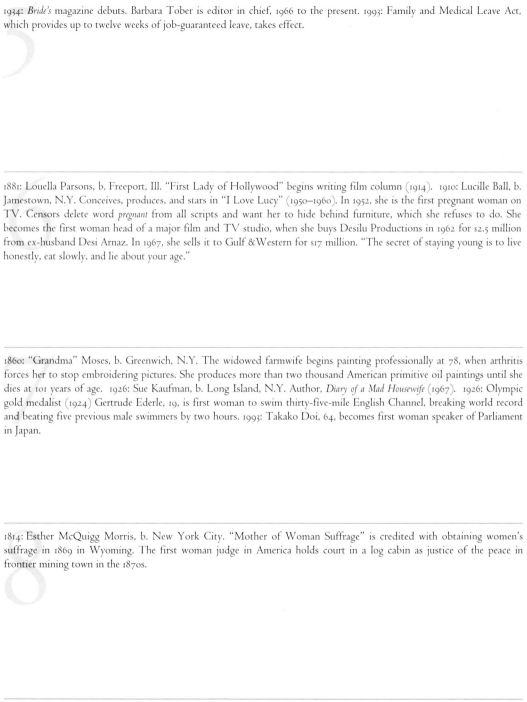

1934: *Bride's* magazine debuts. Barbara Tober is editor in chief, 1966 to the present. 1993: Family and Medical Leave Act, which provides up to twelve weeks of job-guaranteed leave, takes effect.

1881: Louella Parsons, b. Freeport, Ill. "First Lady of Hollywood" begins writing film column (1914). 1910: Lucille Ball, b. Jamestown, N.Y. Conceives, produces, and stars in "I Love Lucy" (1950–1960). In 1952, she is the first pregnant woman on TV. Censors delete word *pregnant* from all scripts and want her to hide behind furniture, which she refuses to do. She becomes the first woman head of a major film and TV studio, when she buys Desilu Productions in 1962 for $2.5 million from ex-husband Desi Arnaz. In 1967, she sells it to Gulf & Western for $17 million. "The secret of staying young is to live honestly, eat slowly, and lie about your age."

1860: "Grandma" Moses, b. Greenwich, N.Y. The widowed farmwife begins painting professionally at 78, when arthritis forces her to stop embroidering pictures. She produces more than two thousand American primitive oil paintings until she dies at 101 years of age. 1926: Sue Kaufman, b. Long Island, N.Y. Author, *Diary of a Mad Housewife* (1967). 1926: Olympic gold medalist (1924) Gertrude Ederle, 19, is first woman to swim thirty-five-mile English Channel, breaking world record and beating five previous male swimmers by two hours. 1993: Takako Doi, 64, becomes first woman speaker of Parliament in Japan.

1814: Esther McQuigg Morris, b. New York City. "Mother of Woman Suffrage" is credited with obtaining women's suffrage in 1869 in Wyoming. The first woman judge in America holds court in a log cabin as justice of the peace in frontier mining town in the 1870s.

9
1963: Whitney Houston, b. Newark, N.J. Her 1985 debut album sells more than fourteen million copies; "Saving All My Love for You" wins a Grammy (1986). First artist to achieve seven consecutive number-one hits, more than the Beatles.

10
1900: Josephine Holt Bay, b. Iowa. First woman head of N.Y. Stock Exchange firm (1956). 1942: Betsey Johnson, b. Wethersfield, Conn. Fashion designer. 1993: Ruth Bader Ginsburg, 60, is sworn in as the second woman and 107th justice of the U.S. Supreme Court. (See Oct. 4.)

11
1897: Louise Bogan, b. Livermore Falls, Maine. First woman consultant in poetry, Library of Congress (1945–1946); work appears in *The New Yorker* over three decades.

12
1859: Katherine Lee Bates, b. Falmouth, Mass. Wellesley graduate writes "America the Beautiful," which becomes commencement tradition. 1876: Mary Roberts Rinehart, b. Pittsburgh, Pa. First war correspondent to report from front lines during WWI. Detective novelist averages one book per year for more than forty years. 1972: Wendy Rue founds the National Assn. for Female Executives (NAFE), which becomes the largest businesswomen's organization in U.S., with more than 250,000 members. 1992: Roxanne Barton Conlin is first woman president of the Assn. of Trial Lawyers of America, founded 1946.

1818: Lucy Stone, b. W. Brookfield, Mass. Leads national Woman's Rights Convention, Worcester, Mass., in 1850. Breaks antimarriage vow at 37 to marry Henry Blackwell, brother of Drs. Elizabeth and Emily Blackwell. Insists on retaining her maiden name; women who follow custom are called "Lucy Stoners." With husband, supports founding of American Suffrage Assn. 1859: Annie Oakley, b. Ohio. "The Peerless Lady Wing-Shot" stars in "Buffalo Bill's Wild West Show" (1885–1902). "Annie Oakley" becomes nickname for punched-out train ticket.

1928: Lina Wertmuller, b. Rome. First woman director Oscar nominee, *Seven Beauties* (1975). 1947: Danielle Steel, b. New York City. Romance author sells more than 150 million books worldwide; averages two books a year; record eleven consecutive books on *New York Times* best-seller list (1983–1989); earns estimated $25 million a year.

Annie Oakley

1885: Edna Ferber, b. Kalamazoo, Mich. Pulitzer Prize for Fiction, *So Big* (1925). 1896: Gerty Radnitz Cori, b. Czechoslovakia. Together with her husband, she receives Nobel Prize for Medicine in 1947. Is made professor of biochemistry the year she is awarded Nobel Prize. 1912: Julia Child, b. Pasadena, Calif. Begins cooking at 36 when she moves to Paris with her husband. It takes ten years to coproduce *Mastering the Art of French Cooking* (1961). Begins "The French Chef" series on PBS-TV in 1963. 1924: Phyllis Stewart Schlafly, b. St. Louis. President, Eagle Forum. 1944: Linda Ellerbee, b. Bryan, Tex. Broadcaster, producer; heads own Lucky Duck Productions. 1950: Princess Anne, b. London.

1947: Rep. Carol Moseley-Braun, b. Chicago. First African-American woman in Senate (D-Ill.), 1993 to the present. Speaking "as the descendant of slaves," she successfully reversed the Senate's sanction of a Confederate flag emblem (1993). 1953: Kathie Lee Gifford, b. Paris. Shares birthday with husband, Frank Gifford (1930). 1958: Madonna (Louise Ciccone), b. Bay City, Mich. "The Material Girl" is CEO of Boy Toy Inc. 1975: Karen Stead, 11, becomes first woman Soap Box Derby winner. 1984: Jaycees admit women members, following U.S. Supreme Court decision.

1893: Mae West, b. Brooklyn. Actress is highest-paid woman in U.S. 1935, earning $481,000; makes her first film at 40. "The best way to hold a man is in your arms." "It's not the men in my life that counts . . . it's the life in my men." "Why don't you come up sometime and see me?" "Mae West" describes inflatable vest life preserver jacket.

1900: Mme. Visaya Pandit, b. India. First woman president, UN General Assembly. 1927: Rosalynn Smith Carter, b. Plains, Ga. First Lady (1977–1981). Campaign adviser; second First Lady to attend cabinet meetings; weekly working lunches with the president. Honorary chair, President's Commission on Mental Health. 1950: Nadine Strossen, b. Jersey City, N.J. First woman president (1991) of American Civil Liberties Union (ACLU).

1814: Mary Ellen Pleasant, b. Philadelphia. "Mother of civil rights in California" sues trolley line when she is refused passage. 1883: Coco Chanel, b. France. Fashion designer revolutionizes women's fashion after WWI with "Chanel look"; creates Chanel No. 5 (her lucky number) perfume (1924). 1948: Tipper Gore, b. Washington, D.C. Wife of VP Al Gore. Second Lady, 1993 to the present. Mental health adviser to the President's Health Task Force. Founded organization for voluntary labeling of explicit music lyrics.

Coco Chanel

20 1973: Women in Film and Television is organized in Hollywood; in New York in 1978.

21 1930: Princess Margaret, b. Scotland.

22 1893: Dorothy Parker, b. Long Beach N.J. Poet, short-story writer; cofounder of the Algonquin Round Table in 1920s. Epitaph: "Excuse my dust." 1984: Diane Sawyer debuts as the first woman cohost on "60 Minutes" (1989); Leslie Stahl files first report on Apr. 19, 1991.

1944: Dr. Antonia C. Novello, b. Puerto Rico. First woman and first Hispanic surgeon general (1990–1993).

1869: Harriet Morrison Irwin becomes the first woman in U.S. to patent an architectural innovation, a hexagonal house in Charlotte, N.C. Her designs increases floor space; synthesize form and function, biology and technology, to be ergonomically correct. 1950: Atty. Edith S. Sampson is the first African-American delegate to UN.

1841: The first three women granted BA degrees in the U.S. graduate from Oberlin Collegiate Institute, Ohio. By 1900, 80% of the colleges, universities, and professional schools in the U.S. admit women. In 1979, more women than men enter college for the first time in U.S. history. By 1993, women constitute 55% of all undergraduates and receive 54% of bachelor degrees. 1927: Althea Gibson, b. Silver, S.C. Tennis pioneer is first African-American to compete and win U.S. Open and Wimbledon (1957–1958). She later becomes the only African-American member of the Ladies' Pro Golf Assn. (LPGA).

1920: The Nineteenth Amendment granting American women in every state the right to vote is ratified after almost a century of struggle. The National American Woman Suffrage Assn., led by Carrie Lane Chapman Catt and Susan B. Anthony, campaigned since 1869 for a woman's right to vote. Catt notes that it has taken 56 referenda to male voters, 480 efforts to get state legislatures to submit suffrage amendment, and 19 successive congressional campaigns. In 1984 more women than men will vote in U.S. for the first time. 1935: Geraldine Ferraro (Zacarro), b. Newburgh, N.Y. First woman VP nominee of a major party, at Democratic National Convention (1984). She retains her maiden name out of respect for her mother. U.S. ambassador to UN Human Rights Commission (1993 to the present). 1970: Women's Strike for Equality on fiftieth anniversary of woman's suffrage, in New York City. 1974: Bella Abzug sponsors bill designating Aug. 26 as "Women's Equality Day" and spearheads National Women's Conference in Houston to set agenda for women (1977).

Women's Equality Day

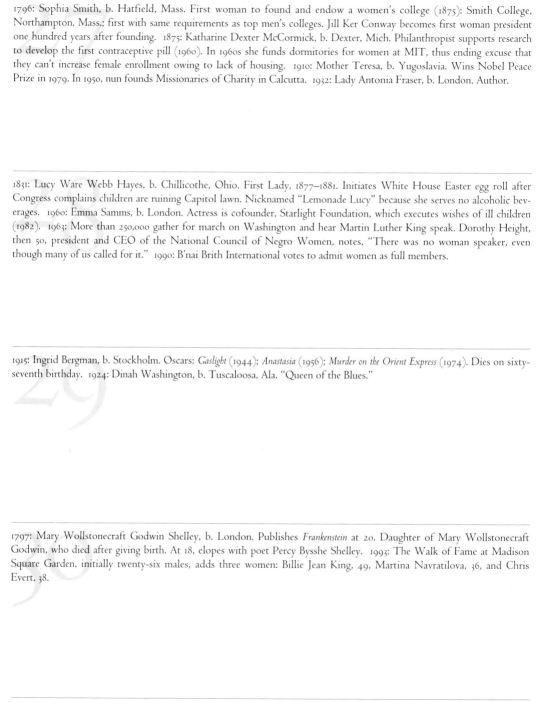

1796: Sophia Smith, b. Hatfield, Mass. First woman to found and endow a women's college (1875): Smith College, Northampton, Mass.; first with same requirements as top men's colleges. Jill Ker Conway becomes first woman president one hundred years after founding. 1875: Katharine Dexter McCormick, b. Dexter, Mich. Philanthropist supports research to develop the first contraceptive pill (1960). In 1960s she funds dormitories for women at MIT, thus ending excuse that they can't increase female enrollment owing to lack of housing. 1910: Mother Teresa, b. Yugoslavia. Wins Nobel Peace Prize in 1979. In 1950, nun founds Missionaries of Charity in Calcutta. 1932: Lady Antonia Fraser, b. London. Author.

1831: Lucy Ware Webb Hayes, b. Chillicothe, Ohio. First Lady, 1877–1881. Initiates White House Easter egg roll after Congress complains children are ruining Capitol lawn. Nicknamed "Lemonade Lucy" because she serves no alcoholic beverages. 1960: Emma Samms, b. London. Actress is cofounder, Starlight Foundation, which executes wishes of ill children (1982). 1963: More than 250,000 gather for march on Washington and hear Martin Luther King speak. Dorothy Height, then 50, president and CEO of the National Council of Negro Women, notes, "There was no woman speaker, even though many of us called for it." 1990: B'nai Brith International votes to admit women as full members.

1915: Ingrid Bergman, b. Stockholm. Oscars: *Gaslight* (1944); *Anastasia* (1956); *Murder on the Orient Express* (1974). Dies on sixty-seventh birthday. 1924: Dinah Washington, b. Tuscaloosa, Ala. "Queen of the Blues."

1797: Mary Wollstonecraft Godwin Shelley, b. London. Publishes *Frankenstein* at 20. Daughter of Mary Wollstonecraft Godwin, who died after giving birth. At 18, elopes with poet Percy Bysshe Shelley. 1993: The Walk of Fame at Madison Square Garden, initially twenty-six males, adds three women: Billie Jean King, 49, Martina Navratilova, 36, and Chris Evert, 38.

1842: Mary Putnam Jacobi, b. London. Physician perseveres to become the first woman admitted to Ecole de Médecine in Paris (1868). Establishes American Medical Women's Assn. (1872). 1870: Maria Montessori, b. Italy. Educator writes *The Montessori Method* (1912), which stresses child's initiative. Opens first school in Rome (1907). 1936: Elizabeth Cowell becomes the first woman announcer on BBC, selected from more than 1,200 applicants. Armine Sandford becomes BBC's first woman TV newscaster on Sept. 30, 1957.

Maria Montessori

SEPTEMBER

1878: Emma M. Nutt becomes the first woman telephone operator in U.S., in Boston. 1933: Ann Richards, b. Lakeview, Tex. First woman elected governor in Tex. (1990 to the present). 1939: Lily Tomlin, b. Detroit, Mich. Comedienne, actress. "The trouble with the rat race is that even if you win, you're still a rat." "If I had known what it was like to have it all, I might have been willing to settle for less." 1961: Dee Dee Myers, b. Valencia, Calif. First woman White House press secretary; deputy assistant to Pres. Bill Clinton (1993 to the present).

1948: Christa McAuliffe, b. Boston. N.H. teacher is selected from eleven thousand applicants in 1985 to be the first citizen in space; dies aboard *Challenger* (1986). 1977: First ten women earn wings as U.S. Air Force pilots. In 1992 federal restriction barring women from combat duty is lifted, and women serve in Desert Storm.

1920: Marguerite Higgins, b. Hong Kong. First woman to win Pulitzer Prize for Foreign Correspondence (1951), for coverage of Korean War, where she is the only woman correspondent; Vietnam War; Berlin and Tokyo bureau chief, *New York Herald Tribune* (1947–1950).

1963: Harvard Business School now accepts women. Eight women enroll in class of 1965; 226 women (28%) enter with class of 1995.

Emma M. Nutt

1950: Cathy Guisewite, b. Dayton, Ohio. Cartoonist. "Cathy," the single career woman, debuts Nov. 22, 1976. Syndicated internationally in more than 1,200 newspapers. President, Guisewite Studio (1991 to the present). Second woman winner of National Cartoonists Society's annual Reuben award (1993).

1860: Jane Addams, b. Cedarville, Ill. Founder, first major settlement house in U.S., Hull House, Chicago (1889). First American woman to receive Nobel Peace Prize (1931). Cofounder (1920), American Civil Liberties Union. 1975: Lynn Povich is *Newsweek*'s first woman senior editor. In 1991, she becomes editor in chief of *Working Woman*, founded 1976.

Jane Addams (*right*)

1925: Laura Ashley, b. Wales. Fashion designer with worldwide chain of stores. 1974: First Sex Crimes Prosecution Unit in the U.S. is established in New York City District Attorney's Office, led by Leslie Crocker Snyder until 1976; she is succeeded in 1976 by Linda Fairstein. 1991: Tailhook convention in Las Vegas. Navy helicopter pilot Lt. Paula Coughlin's persistent complaints start investigation. Barbara Spyridon Pope, assistant secretary and the navy's highest-ranking woman civilian in navy history, is asked to approve a report of the three-day scandal. She refuses and offers resignation, which sparks a more thorough investigation. The Pentagon reports 140 cases of misconduct. 1993: Dr. Joycelyn Elders, 57-year-old pediatrician, is confirmed as the first African-American and second woman surgeon general, succeeding Dr. Antonia Novello.

1921: Margaret Gorman, 15, becomes the first Miss America, of eight contestants in Atlantic City, N.J. By 1990s, $10 million in scholarship grants is available annually to contestants at local, state, and national levels; title carries $35,000 scholarship. 1932: Patsy Cline, b. Winchester, Va. "Queen of Country Music." First woman solo performer inducted into Country Music Hall of Fame (1973). By 1993, eight women are inducted.

Margaret Gorman

9 1986: Barneys women's store opens in New York City. In 1923, Mrs. Bertha Pressman sold her engagement ring to raise capital for husband Barney's first men's clothing store. By 1993, there are sixteen stores in U.S. and Japan.

10 1975: Harvard College adopts policy of equal admission for women undergraduate students. Yale accepted women undergraduates in 1969; Princeton in 1970; Brown in 1971; Dartmouth in 1972; and Columbia College, the last Ivy League holdout, in 1983, where women will lead the first coed graduating class as valedictorian and salutatorian.

11 1869: Leonora Barkaloo is the first woman admitted to a law school, Washington Univ. New York Univ. Law School will admit women in 1890; Yale in 1918; Columbia in 1927; Harvard in 1950. From 1970 to 1993, the number of women awarded law degrees in U.S. increases to 44% from 5%. 1911: Alice Tully, b. Corning, N.Y. Operatic soprano funds hall for chamber music recitals at Lincoln Center, New York City.

12 1910: Alice Stebbins Wells, a former social worker, becomes the first woman police officer in U.S., in Los Angeles. As a result of her efforts, by 1916, seventeen police departments employ policewomen. 1992: Royal Air Force bandswomen debut at Changing of the Guard ceremony at Buckingham Palace, ending 155-year-old male tradition.

1993: Playing pivotal roles behind the historic Israel-Palestine Liberation Organization (PLO) White House meeting are Palestinian spokeswoman Hanan Ashrawi and Marianne Heiberg, a scholar on living conditions in the Occupied Territories and wife of the Norwegian foreign minister.

1830: Emily Edson Briggs, b. Burton, Ohio. First woman White House correspondent (1861), during Lincoln's administration. First president Women's National Press Assn. (1882). 1879: Margaret Higgins Sanger, b. Corning, N.Y.; sixth of eleven children. In 1916 founds first U.S. birth control clinic. Cofounder and first president, International Planned Parenthood (1952). 1882: Winnifred Huck, b. Chicago. In 1921, when her Ill. congressman father dies, she establishes precedent of a relative seeking to fill unexpired term; in 1922, she is elected in her own right. 1897: Margaret Fogarty Rudkin, b. New York City. Starts Pepperidge Farm bakeries at 40, with home-baked bread in her Fairfield, Conn., home, named after an old pepperidge tree. In 1960 she sells the business to Campbell Soup Co. for stock worth $28 million. 1921: Constance Baker Motley, b. New Haven, Conn. First woman, Manhattan, N.Y., borough president (1965). First African-American woman federal court judge (1966). As associate counsel, NAACP Legal Defense Fund (for twenty years), she argues Charlayne Hunter-Gault's case to enter Univ. of Ga. (1961).

Margaret Higgins Sanger

1881: Lena Madeson Phillips, b. Nicholasville, Ky. Lawyer is founder (1919) of National and International Federation of Business and Professional Women's Clubs (BPW). 1890: Dame Agatha Christie, b. England. World's best-selling mystery writer creates sleuth Miss Jane Marple; her mysteries sell almost two billion copies in forty-four languages. She advises, "Marry an anthropologist. The older you get, the more interested he becomes." Her second husband, eighteen years her junior, is an anthropologist. She begins earning her living as a writer after her first husband leaves her for a younger woman. 1945: Jessye Norman, b. Augusta, Ga. Opera singer, Metropolitan Opera, N.Y., 1983 to the present.

1974: Mary Louise Smith, of Iowa, is first woman chair, Republican National Committee. First woman of any party to organize and call to order a national convention (1976). 1976: Episcopal Church's general convention approves ordination of women.

1953: Sophie Tucker, 69, "last of the red-hot mamas," is the first woman honored at a Friar's Club roast, New York City. Liza Minnelli is first woman member in New York City (1988); by 1993, there are 125 women among 1,400 members. 1983: Vanessa Williams, 21, becomes the first African-American Miss America in sixty-two-year history. She resigns in July after negative publicity and makes comeback as award-winning recording star and performer.

1905: Agnes De Mille, b. New York City. Innovative American dancer-author makes "ballet" a household word. 1976: Beatrice Fitzpatrick establishes American Women's Economic Development Corp. (AWED), the first organization to provide training and support for women business owners nationwide. In 1976, women represent 4% of business owners; by 1987, more than 30%. Today, women-owned businesses employ more people than the *Fortune* 500 companies combined. It is projected that by the year 2000, women will own 40%–50% of all U.S. businesses.

1951: Joan Lunden, b. Sacramento, Calif. Cohost, "Good Morning America" (1980 to the present). 1970: "Mary Tyler Moore Show" debuts as single woman's best friend on Saturday night television. 1990: Cantors' Assembly of Conservative movement of Judaism votes to admit women.

1973: Billie Jean King, 29, defeats Bobby Riggs, 55 ("No broad can beat me") in "Battle of the Sexes" tennis match to win $100,000, the largest purse paid for single tennis match. A record 30,472 people are at the Houston Astrodome; the match remains tennis's most watched TV event.

1884: Ethel Andrus, b. San Francisco. Founder (1958), American Assn. of Retired Persons (AARP). First woman high school principal in Calif. (1916). 1993: Ann Moore becomes the first woman president of *People* magazine.

1656: First women jurors, in Md. 1880: Dame Christabel Pankhurst, b. England. With mother, Emmeline, founds the British suffragette movement. Jailed several times, she declares, "If it would get us the vote, I should be ready to go to prison again at any time."

1838: Victoria Chaflin Woodhull, b. Homer, Ohio. First woman candidate for U.S. presidency (1872). With sister, first women members of N.Y. Stock Exchange (1870s). 1863: Dr. Mary Church Terrell, b. Memphis, Tenn. First president, National Assn. of Colored Women (1896–1901). At 85, she integrates American Assn. of University Women; at 89, she leads pickets to desegregate Washington, D.C., lunchrooms. 1899: Louise Nevelson, b. Russia. Pioneers large environmental sculptures.

Victoria Chaflin Woodhull

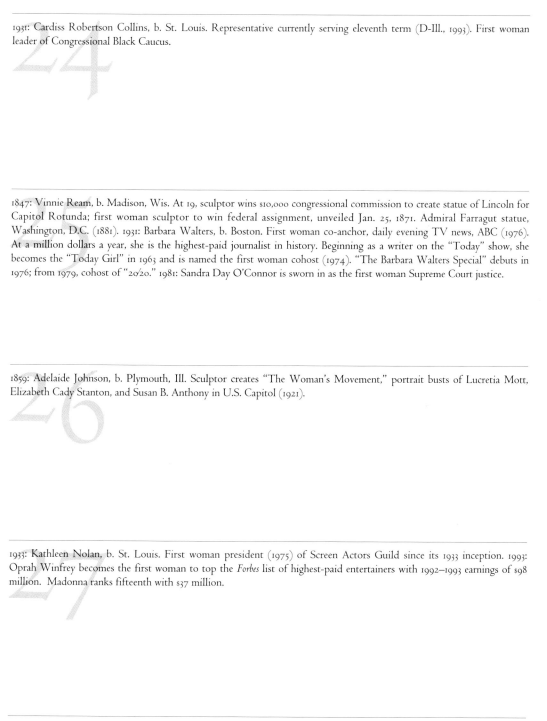

1931: Cardiss Robertson Collins, b. St. Louis. Representative currently serving eleventh term (D-Ill., 1993). First woman leader of Congressional Black Caucus.

1847: Vinnie Ream, b. Madison, Wis. At 19, sculptor wins $10,000 congressional commission to create statue of Lincoln for Capitol Rotunda; first woman sculptor to win federal assignment, unveiled Jan. 25, 1871. Admiral Farragut statue, Washington, D.C. (1881). 1931: Barbara Walters, b. Boston. First woman co-anchor, daily evening TV news, ABC (1976). At a million dollars a year, she is the highest-paid journalist in history. Beginning as a writer on the "Today" show, she becomes the "Today Girl" in 1963 and is named the first woman cohost (1974). "The Barbara Walters Special" debuts in 1976; from 1979, cohost of "20/20." 1981: Sandra Day O'Connor is sworn in as the first woman Supreme Court justice.

1859: Adelaide Johnson, b. Plymouth, Ill. Sculptor creates "The Woman's Movement," portrait busts of Lucretia Mott, Elizabeth Cady Stanton, and Susan B. Anthony in U.S. Capitol (1921).

1933: Kathleen Nolan, b. St. Louis. First woman president (1975) of Screen Actors Guild since its 1933 inception. 1993: Oprah Winfrey becomes the first woman to top the *Forbes* list of highest-paid entertainers with 1992–1993 earnings of $98 million. Madonna ranks fifteenth with $37 million.

1839: Frances Elizabeth Willard, b. Churchville, N.Y. First woman college president, Evanston College for Ladies, Ill. (1871). First president, National Council of Women (1888). First woman to have her statue, by Helen Mears, in U.S. Capitol (1905). 1881: Eleonora Sears, b. Boston. First woman to play polo against men (1910), she causes a scandal by wearing trousers. Later she makes headlines when she dares to roll up her sleeves during a tennis match. 1993: Hillary Rodham Clinton, as head of the president's American Health Security Act, becomes the third First Lady to testify before Congress, as lead-off witness, and the first to speak as an advocate and the architect of a major piece of legislation. (Eleanor Roosevelt testified on the problems of migrant labor in the 1940s and Rosalynn Carter spoke on mental health reform in the 1970s.)

1988: Stacy Allison of Portland, Oreg., becomes first U.S. woman (and seventh woman) to reach summit of Mt. Everest.

1980: The International Alliance of professional and executive women's networks is founded; by 1986, has members in North America, Europe, and Asia.

Hillary Rodham Clinton

O C T O B E R

1953: Grete Waitz, b. Oslo. Track athlete wins New York City Marathon record nine times (1978–1988). One woman entered the first race in 1970; 6,059 run in 1993. 1987: California passes law not to permit state tax deductions for business expenses incurred at clubs that discriminate against women and minorities. 1993: Pulitzer Prize winner Rita Dove, 40, replaces Mona Van Duyn, 72, as U.S. poet laureate. First African-American woman and youngest honoree. Pulitzer Prize for Poetry about her grandparents (1987). "Poetry is actually a witness for life."

1885: Ruth Bryan Rohde, b. Jacksonville, Ill. Daughter of William Jennings Bryan. First woman to serve on major congressional committee, Foreign Affairs. First woman appointed to major diplomatic post (1933), envoy to Denmark. 1948: Donna (Faske) Karan, b. Long Island, N.Y. Fashion designer trains with Anne Klein (1974–1984); on May 3, 1985, launches own label—Donna Karan New York. 1949: Annie Leibovitz, b. New York City. Photographer.

1891: "Baby Ruth" Cleveland, b. New York City. Candy bar is named for First Daughter, during Pres. Cleveland's second term. 1922: Rebecca Ann Latimer Felton, 87, of Cartersville, Ga., is appointed first woman U.S. senator. 1922: Venita Walker VanCaspel, b. Sweetwater, Okla. In 1968 becomes first woman member of Pacific Stock Exchange, San Francisco.

1976: Barbara Walters becomes the first woman co-anchor of evening news, at ABC. In 1993 Connie Chung will be second, at CBS. 1993: Ruth Bader Ginsburg joins Supreme Court as the second woman and 107th justice. She transfers to Columbia Law from Harvard to join her husband; graduates first in class and is on the *Law Review* (1959). In 1972 she will become Columbia Law's first tenured woman faculty member. As women's rights advocate, she wins five (of six) landmark cases before the Supreme Court and expands the scope of the equal-protection clause by suing on behalf of men in some cases. After accepting Pres. Clinton's nomination, she pays tribute to her mother who died the night before her high school graduation: "I pray that I may be all that she would have been had she lived in a age when women could aspire and achieve, and daughters are cherished as much as sons."

Barbara Walters

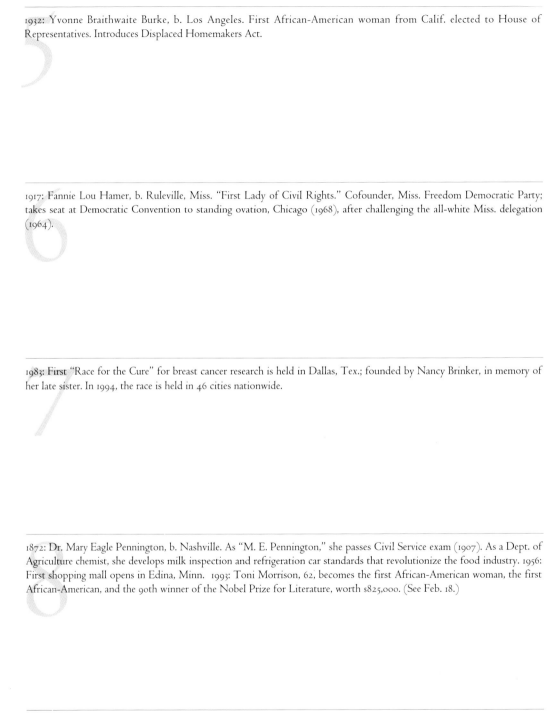

5
1932: Yvonne Braithwaite Burke, b. Los Angeles. First African-American woman from Calif. elected to House of Representatives. Introduces Displaced Homemakers Act.

6
1917: Fannie Lou Hamer, b. Ruleville, Miss. "First Lady of Civil Rights." Cofounder, Miss. Freedom Democratic Party; takes seat at Democratic Convention to standing ovation, Chicago (1968), after challenging the all-white Miss. delegation (1964).

7
1983: First "Race for the Cure" for breast cancer research is held in Dallas, Tex.; founded by Nancy Brinker, in memory of her late sister. In 1994, the race is held in 46 cities nationwide.

8
1872: Dr. Mary Eagle Pennington, b. Nashville. As "M. E. Pennington," she passes Civil Service exam (1907). As a Dept. of Agriculture chemist, she develops milk inspection and refrigeration car standards that revolutionize the food industry. 1956: First shopping mall opens in Edina, Minn. 1993: Toni Morrison, 62, becomes the first African-American woman, the first African-American, and the 90th winner of the Nobel Prize for Literature, worth $825,000. (See Feb. 18.)

9 1985: Lillian Vernon is named the first "Woman of the Year" by the Women's Direct Response Group, founded 1981. In 1961, she starts the mail-order business on her kitchen table; publishes first catalog in 1954; in 1987 company goes public.

10 1983: Botanist Barbara McClintock receives Nobel Prize for Chemistry. Six women have become Nobel laureates in science, among more than 350 winners since 1901, when prizes were inaugurated. 1991: Dr. Geraldine Morrow, from Anchorage, Alaska, is installed as the first woman president of the American Dental Assn., founded 1858.

11 1884: Eleanor Roosevelt, b. New York City. First Lady, 1933–1945. First to give her own news conference (1933); only women reporters and photographers are welcome, thus creating work for women during Depression. First to testify before Senate committee. First to serve as delegate to UN General Assembly. "No one can make you feel inferior without your consent." 1950: Patty Murray, b. Bothell, Wash. Senator (D-Wash.), 1993 to the present. Campaigns as "a mom in tennis shoes" with the support of ten thousand volunteers. 1972: The Ms. Foundation for Women is founded. 1984: Dr. Kathryn D. Sullivan, 33, is the first U.S. woman astronaut to "walk" in space, during *Challenger* flight. 1994: On the 110th anniversary of Eleanor Roosevelt's birthday, the first public statue of an American woman ever commissioned for a city park is unveiled in Riverside Park, New York City. Boston sculptor Penelope Jencks creates the statue.

Eleanor Roosevelt

1923: Jean Nidetch, b. Brooklyn. Founds Weight Watchers in 1963; sells to H. J. Heinz Co. for $72 million in 1979. 1991: Senate hearings on confirmation of Clarence Thomas to the Supreme Court and sexual-harassment charges by Prof. Anita Hill are televised. The next year EEOC sexual-harassment complaints double to almost twelve thousand.

1969: Nancy Kerrigan, b. Stoneham, Mass. On February 23, 1994 Olympic figure skater won silver medal; Oksana Baiul, 16, of Ukraine, won gold medal by the narrowest margin in Olympic history. 1993: FBI appoints Burdena Pasenelli as the first woman assistant director; she was first woman special agent in charge of a field office, in Anchorage, Alaska. Women, first admitted in 1972, now number 1,200 of the FBI's 10,300 agents, or 11.5%.

1896: Lillian Gish, b. Springfield, Ohio. "First Lady of the Screen." She bequeaths Museum of Modern Art's film department a trust fund of $1.2 million.

1872: Edith Bolling Galt Wilson, b. Wytheville, Va. First Lady, 1915–1921. After Pres. Wilson's 1919 stroke, she unofficially runs the country. 1906: Alicia Patterson, b. Chicago. Cofounder, *Newsday* (1940); largest suburban newspaper in U.S. 1943: Penny Marshall, b. New York City. Actress. Director, *Big* (1988); *A League of Their Own* (1992).

Lillian Gish

1925: Angela Lansbury, b. London. Star of musical theater. Since 1984 she plays lead in "Murder, She Wrote." 1993: Julia Child, 81, becomes the first woman inducted into the Culinary Institute of America's Hall of Fame. Twenty percent of the students at the institute are now women.

1868: Sophia Gregoria Hayden, b. Chile. First woman architecture student at MIT (1886). Wins first place in design competition for Women's Building at Chicago Exposition (1891). 1956: Dr. Mae C. Jemison, b. Decatur, Ala. First African-American woman in space (1992). Physician is selected for astronaut training program (1987); one of fifteen candidates of two thousand qualified applicants. NASA's ninety-two astronauts now include sixteen women.

1836: Ellen Scripps, b. London. Founder, Scripps College for Women (1926). Philanthropist was cofounder of Scripps-Howard newspaper chain. 1923: Melina Mercouri, b. Athens. Actress wins seat in Greek Parliament (1977 to 1994); serves as minister of culture and sciences (1981–1990). 1919: Violeta Barrios de Chamorro, b. Nicaragua. In 1990 becomes first elected woman president of a Central American nation. 1950: Wendy Wasserstein, b. Brooklyn. Playwright wins Pulitzer Prize and Tony Award for *The Heidi Chronicles* (1988). "This is hard work." In 1993, *The Sisters Rosensweig* opens. 1951: Terry McMillan, b. Pt. Huron, Mich. She makes her living at word processing until her first novel, *Mama*, is published, 1987. Her third novel, *Waiting to Exhale* (1992), is best-seller; paperback rights sell for $2.64 million. 1956: Martina Navratilova, b. Czechoslovakia. She defects from Czechoslovakia at 19 and goes on to win 165 singles titles (1973–1993), including an unprecedented nine at Wimbledon and more match victories (165) than any player in the history of the sport. By 1991, she has earned more than $19 million. She plans to retire after the 1994 season.

1858: Alice McLellan Birney, b. Marietta, Ga. Founder, first president (1897), Parent-Teacher Assn. (PTA). 1868: Bertha Knight Landes, b. Ware, Mass. First woman mayor (1926–1928) of a major U.S. city (Seattle). 1936: Johnnetta Betsch Cole, b. Jacksonville, Fla. In 1987, she is named the first African-American woman president of Spelman College for women, 196 years after it is founded. At her inauguration, Camille and Bill Cosby donate $20 million. 1987: Stock market analyst Elaine Garzarelli predicted this historic stock market crash the week before.

1904: Enolia P. McMillan, b. Willow Grove, Pa. At 79, the educator is elected the first woman president of the National Assn. for the Advancement of Colored People (NAACP, founded 1909). 1945: Nina Hirschfeld, b. New York City. On her birth, Al Hirschfeld, her father and noted theatrical caricaturist, hides her name, Nina, in his pen drawings. "Finding the Ninas" becomes a national pastime; next to his signature is the number of Ninas in the drawing.

Caricature of Lily Tomlin, in which Nina Hirschfeld's name appears

1920: Frieda Loehmann opens discount designer clothing store beneath her Brooklyn apartment. 1940: Frances FitzGerald, b. New York City. Pulitzer Prize, *Fire in the Lake,* book about Vietnam (1972). 1958: First women are admitted to the British House of Lords.

1921: The Assocation of Junior Leagues International is established by Mary Harriman. By 1994, membership in 283 leagues worldwide includes almost 300,000 women volunteers. 1943: Catherine Deneuve, b. Paris. Actress.

1844: Sarah Bernhardt, b. Paris. "The Divine Sarah" makes her screen debut at 56 and continues to perform after she loses a leg in stage accident. She is the first woman to wear trousers as feminine apparel (1876). 1942: Anita Roddick, b. Sussex, England. Opens The Body Shop in Brighton, England, in 1976 with $6,500 bank loan. Company goes public in 1984; opens in U.S. in 1988. In 1993, the chain has more than one thousand stores in forty-five countries. She is one of the five richest women in England. 1993: Nannerl O. Keohane, 53, former president of Wellesley College, is inaugurated as president of Duke Univ.

1788: Sara Josepha Hale, b. Newport, N.H. In 1822, the widow with five children begins her literary career as editor of *Godey's Lady's Book*, the most popular magazine of its time. In 1830 she writes "Mary Had a Little Lamb." 1830: Belva Lockwood, b, Royalton, N.Y. First woman lawyer admitted to practice before the Supreme Court (1879). Runs for president in 1884 on the National Equal Rights ticket. In 1872, she drafts landmark bill giving women government workers equal pay for equal work. 1981: The National Coalition of 100 Black Women leadership forum is founded by Jewell Jackson McCabe. By 1993, there are more than eight thousand members in thirty states.

1989: Violin prodigy Midori celebrates her eighteenth birthday with Carnegie Hall debut.

Belva Lockwood

1874: Abby Rockefeller, b. Providence, R.I. Cofounder (1929), Museum of Modern Art (MOMA). 1947: Hillary Rodham Clinton, b. Chicago. First Lady, 1993 to the present. First to establish office in West Wing; first appointed by president to head task force on health-care reform to craft the U.S.'s first comprehensive health-care program. Designated a de facto federal official. Bans smoking from White House. First chair of the American Bar Assn.'s Commission on Women in the Legal Profession. Voted one of the nation's top one hundred lawyers (1988, 1991). Wellesley graduate (1969); president of student body and the first student to deliver commencement speech. Upon graduating Yale Law, where she met the president, she is one of three women among forty-three lawyers on the House Judiciary Committee's investigation into Watergate. 1986: American Craft Museum, founded by Aileen Osborn Webb (1956), as the world's first modern craft museum, opens across from MOMA, New York City.

1940: Maxine Hong Kingston, b. Stockton, Calif. *The Woman Warrior* (1977), autobiography of Chinese-American female experience. 1950: Fran Lebowitz, b. Morristown, N.J. Humorist. "Life is something to do when you can't get to sleep." 1981: C. Rose Harper, an innovative mailing-list expert, becomes first woman chair of the Direct Marketing Assn., founded 1917. First woman inducted into DMA Hall of Fame (1985).

1907: Edith Head, b. Los Angeles. First woman to head design department of major film studio (Paramount, 1938). A total of thirty-five Oscar nominations; champion Oscar winner: eight. Designs uniforms for Pan Am, UN. **1939:** Jane Alexander, b. Boston. Actress is first performer (1993 to the present) to chair the National Endowment for the Arts (NEA). **1967:** Julia Roberts, b. Smyrna, Ga. At 26, she is the highest-paid actress in Hollywood: more than $8 million a film. **1987:** Dawn Steel becomes the first woman president of Columbia Pictures.

1917: The Women's National Book Assn. is organized at Sherwood's Book Store in lower Manhattan by women booksellers barred from membership in all-male Bookseller's League; by 1993 there are one thousand members worldwide. **1966:** National Organization for Women (NOW) is formed.

1877: Irma Van Starkloff Rombauer, b. St. Louis. Author, *The Joy of Cooking*. When she marries, her husband teaches her to cook. Privately publishes book with five hundred family recipes (1931).

1816: Josephine Newcomb, b. Baltimore. Funds ($3.5 million) and founds H. Sophie Newcomb Memorial College for Women, New Orleans. (1887). First independent women's college connected to men's college, Tulane. **1854:** The 128 female U.S. postmasters receive the same pay as men; first profession to establish pay equity. **1860:** Juliette "Daisy" Gordon Low, b. Savannah, Ga. Widowed at 45, she founds Girl Scouts USA in 1912, in Savannah; president until 1920. In 1993 membership reaches 2.6 million. **1950:** Jane Pauley, b. Indianapolis. Broadcaster.

Halloween

N O V E M B E R

1848: First medical school for women, the Boston Female Medical School, opens with twelve students; merges with Boston Univ. in 1874, to become one of the first coed medical schools in the world. 1945: Johnson Publishing premieres *Ebony*. Company was founded in 1942 when founder pawned his mother's furniture for $500; now the second-largest African-American–owned company in U.S. Daughter Linda Johnson Rice becomes president and CEO in 1987. Wife and cofounder Eunice W. Johnson is secretary-treasurer.

1896: The first Avon catalog is mailed, ten years after the company is founded with one door-to-door saleslady, Persis F. Eames Albee, 50, of Winchester, N.H. (1886). Today, there are 1.7 million Avon ladies; the world's largest employer of women.

1913: Mary Phelps Jacob rebels against corsets and patents an early "bra" made from stitching hankies together with ribbons; sells design for $1,500. 1953: Roseanne Barr Arnold, b. Salt Lake City. "Domestic goddess" stars in "Roseanne" (1988 to the present); in 1993 wins an Emmy. 1992: Election Day; In this year's elections, 54% of the voters are women. The number of women elected to the House of Representatives doubles to 47 (of 435); that of women senators triples to 6 (of 100). Three women state governors are elected (of 50).

1914: First fashion show is held in New York City by *Vogue*. 1914: Charles Miller names peanut-butter candy for his aunt, Mary Jane. 1986: Election Day: Barbara Mikulski becomes first Democratic woman senator not preceded by spouse, Md. (1987–the present). Kay Orr becomes first Republican governor in U.S. history, Nebr. (1987–1991). Both beat female opponents.

Mrs. P.F.E. Albee, the first Avon Lady

5 1857: Ida M. Tarbell, b. Erie County, Pa. First woman investigative reporter encourages federal investigation of Standard Oil, which leads to breakup of company. 1991: Dr. Antoinette Eaton becomes first woman president of American Acad. of Pediatrics, founded in 1930; today almost 40% of the members are women.

6 1990: Election Day: Women governors are elected in three states: Joan Finney (D-Kans.); Barbara Roberts (D-Oreg.); Ann Richards (D-Tex.). Sharon Pratt Dixon becomes the first woman mayor of Washington, D.C. 1993: Dr. Barbara Ross-Lee, 51, is the first African-American woman dean of a U.S. medical school, Ohio Univ. College of Osteopathic Medicine in Athens.

1867: Marie (Sklodowska) Curie, b. Poland. Nobel Prize for Physics, with husband, Pierre, for radium discovery, 1903. Following his death in 1906, the 39-year-old widow wins Nobel Prize for Chemistry. First woman professor at the Sorbonne in 1906; she is appointed to late husband's position. In 1934 she dies of leukemia as result of overexposure to radiation. 1881: Cissy Medill Patterson, b. Chicago. In 1934 becomes first woman publisher of metro daily newspaper, *Washington Herald* (1934). 1937: Mary Travers, b. Louisville, Ky. Folksinger with Peter, Paul, and Mary. 1983: Nancy Cardwell becomes first woman national news editor at *The Wall Street Journal*.

1900: Margaret Mitchell, b. Atlanta, Ga. In 1936 she wins Pulitzer Prize for her only book, *Gone With the Wind*, which she has written sporadically for ten years. It becomes the best-selling novel in U.S. up to that time. Film will win ten Oscars (1940). It has been seen in theaters by more people (199 million) than any other film. She dies on her forty-ninth birthday after being hit by a taxi. 1909: Katharine Hepburn, b. Hartford, Conn. Only person to win four Oscars in starring role; twelve nominations. 1947: Dr. Margaret Rhea Seddon, b. Tenn. First woman to receive full rank of astronaut (1979); in 1985, first space mission. 1993: Ellen Futter, 43, becomes the first woman president of 124-year-old American Museum of Natural History, New York City. At 30, as president of Barnard College, she is the youngest person to head a major university. First woman chair, board of directors, N.Y. Federal Reserve Bank.

Katharine Hepburn

1871: Florence Sabin, b. Central City, Colo. Anatomist is first woman on Johns Hopkins Medical School faculty (1902); first full professor (1917). In 1925 becomes first woman accepted into National Academy of Sciences. 1928: Anne Sexton, b. Newton, Mass. Pulitzer Prize for Poetry (1966).

1972: Betsy Plank is elected first woman president of the Public Relations Society of America, founded 1947. By 1993, women make up 56% of PRSA membership.

1744: Abigail Smith Adams, b. Weymouth, Mass. Mother of Pres. John Quincy Adams. First Lady, 1799–1801. In 1776, she writes to husband John, "Remember the Ladies, and be more generous and favorable to them than your ancestors. Do not put such unlimited power into the hands of the husbands. . . ." 1979: Bethune Museum and Archives is established in Washington, D.C., as center for African-American women's history. 1993: The Vietnam Women's Memorial by sculptor Glenna Goodacre is dedicated in Washington, D.C. The bronze statue depicts three women caring for a wounded soldier. Diane Carlson Evans, a former army combat nurse, conceives the project and campaigns for more than a decade, raising $4 million in donations, to honor the 265,000 women who served during the Vietnam era. 1993: Mary G. Berner, publisher, *TV Guide*, and Sheri Colonel, agency executive, are the first women under 40 inducted into new Hall of Achievement of American Advertising Federation.

Veterans Day

Abigail Smith Adams

1815: Elizabeth Cady Stanton, b. Johnstown, N.Y. After raising seven children, she leads first Women's Rights Convention in her hometown, Seneca Falls, N.Y. (1948). Cofounds women's rights movement with Lucretia Mott. Citing eighteen legal inequities, it formally demands the vote—a first. First president, National Woman's Suffrage Assn. (1869–1890). "We hold these truths to be self-evident, that all men and women are created equal." 1929: Princess Grace (Kelly) of Monaco, b. Philadelphia. She meets Prince Rainier III while filming *To Catch a Thief* on the Riviera (1955) and, 1956, marries him. 1961: Nadia Comaneci, b. Romania. First gymnast to score perfect ten at Olympics (1976).

1949: Whoopi Goldberg, b. New York City. Best Supporting Actress Oscar for *Ghost* (1989); second African-American woman, fifty-one years after Hattie McDaniel. In 1993 she receives $8 million to star in *Sister Act 2.* 1990: Martha S. Pope is first woman sergeant at arms of U.S. Senate.

1889: Nellie Bly, 22, *New York World* reporter, sets sail from N.Y. to beat Phileas Fogg's "round-the-world in 80 days" record in Jules Verne's 1873 novel. She finishes trip in seventy-two days, six hours, eleven minutes. 1946: Emily Greene Balch is awarded Nobel Prize. Cofounder (1915), Women's International League for Peace and Freedom, The Hague. 1988: "Murphy Brown," starring Candice Bergen, premieres.

SHE'S BROKEN EVERY RECORD!

1887: Marianne Moore, b. St. Louis. In 1951 wins Pulitzer Prize for Poetry. 1887: Georgia O'Keeffe, b. Sun Prairie, Wis. Artist. 1949: Sara Lee Bakery opens, named for owner's daughter. Becomes second-largest corporation in the world named for a daughter; the first is Mercedes-Benz in 1926 and Wendy's is the third, founded on this day in 1969. ("Barbie" doll is named for inventor Ruth Handler's daughter, 1959; "Tootsie" Roll candy used owner's pet name for his daughter, 1896; "Chunky" was named after owner's baby granddaughter, 1930s.) 1993: "Star Trek" debuts its first woman Ferengi, the species that enjoys making money—lots of it.

1899: Mary Margaret McBride, b. Paris, Mo. Pioneers modern talk show on radio (1934–1956); seventy-five thousand fans applaud her fifteenth anniversary at Yankee Stadium. 1993: Bureau of Labor Statistics commissioner Katharine Abraham announces the first major change in the unemployment rate monthly survey in fifty years, more accurately counting women as workers rather than housewives.

1880: First three British women graduates receive BA degrees from London Univ. 1943: Lauren Hutton, b. Charleston, S.C. At 30, then modeling's absolute limit, she signs major cosmetics contract; she is the first mature model to sign another cosmetics contract at 50. 1970: The Feminist Press is established. 1988: Benazir Bhutto, 35, is first woman leader of an Islamic country, prime minister of Pakistan; dismissed after twenty months; reelected (1993 to the present).

1857: Rose Knox, b. Mansfield, Ohio. Cofounder, Knox Gelatin Co. (1890). Following husband's death, she leads company "in a woman's way" (1908–1947). Initiates five-day workweek, two-week vacation, sick leave. *Colliers* names her "America's foremost woman industrialist." 1910: Suffragettes attack British House of Commons; 119 are arrested. 1939: Margaret Atwood, b. Ottawa, Canada. Author, *The Handmaid's Tale* (1966); *The Robber Bride* (1993). 1977: First National Women's Conference, Houston; largest meeting since Seneca Falls, N.Y., convention of 1848. More than 1,400 delegates advocate passage of Equal Rights Amendment. Betty Friedan is keynoter.

1917: Indira Gandhi, b. India. Prime Minister of India, 1966–1977; 1978–1984, assassinated by Sikhs. 1926: Jeane (Jordan) Kirkpatrick, b. Duncan, Okla. First woman U.S. ambassador to UN (1981–1985). 1962: Jodie Foster, b. Los Angeles. Actress, director. Oscar, *The Accused* (1989).

Indira Gandhi

1858: Selma Lagerlöf, b. Sweden. First woman Nobel Prize for Literature (1909). 1970: "Wall Street Week" debuts on PBS-TV; created by Anne Truax Darlington.

1929: Marilyn French, b. New York City. Author, *The Women's Room* (1977). 1953: Tina Brown, b. Maidenhead, England. Editor, *The New Yorker* (1992 to the present); editor in chief, *Vanity Fair* (1984–1992). In 1978 she was named Britain's Most Promising Female Journalist of the Year.

1943: Billy Jean (Moffitt) King, b. Long Beach, Calif. She wins the most Grand Slam titles for an American, thirty-nine; including a record twenty Wimbledon titles (1961–1979). In 1971, she becomes first woman athlete to win $100,000 in a year. Founds Women's Tennis Assn. in 1973, the Women's Sports Foundation in 1974, and Women's Pro Softball League in 1975.

1882: Helen Reid, b. Appleton, Wis. VP, publisher, *New York Herald Tribune* (1924–1944). In the 1940s, *Tribune* has the most women staffers of any U.S. daily. 1993: Catalyst, a research organization for women founded by Felice Schwartz in 1962, reports in its Census of Female Directors that there are now five hundred women directors (up from forty-eight in 1977). Women now hold 6.2% of corporate directorships, and 52.6% of *Fortune* 500 and service companies now have female directors.

1974: *BusinessWeek* publishes its first feature on corporate women, "Up the Ladder, Finally." 1993: Sarah Brady has championed the Brady bill, passed by Congress today, with mandatory five-day waiting period for the purchase of handguns, after seven-year battle. The bill is named for her husband, who was Pres. Reagan's press secretary and in 1981 was seriously wounded in assassination attempt.

1865: Kate Gleason, b. Rochester, N.Y. Becomes the first woman president of a national bank (in Rochester, 1917–1919), after the bank president resigns to serve in WWI. First woman student, Cornell College of Engineering. In 1913 she designs the first affordable mass-produced housing "development," in East Rochester. 1895: Helen Hooven Santmyer, b. Xenia, Ohio. At 89, in 1984, her fourth book, . . . *And Ladies of the Club*, becomes a best-seller.

Helen Reid

1863: Thanksgiving Day is celebrated for the first time as a national holiday, thanks to Sarah Josepha Hale, who lobbied Pres. Abraham Lincoln. 1941: Tina Turner, b. Nutbush, Tenn. Singer. 1954: First TV Dinner (turkey) is marketed on Thanksgiving Day. Betty Cronin, a bacteriologist at Swanson, creates the first frozen meal in an aluminum tray, which will be inducted into the Smithsonian collection (1987). More than ten million sold its first year. Previously, American housewives spent an average of one and a half hours preparing dinner.

1937: Gail Sheehy, b. Mamaroneck, N.Y. Author, *Passages* (1976); *The Silent Passage: Menopause* (1992).

1858: The Young Women's Christian Association (YWCA) of the USA is founded by thirty-five women. 1881: The American Association of University Women (AAUW) is established. 1893: Today ninety thousand women vote in New Zealand, the first nation to grant women the right to vote.

1832: Louisa May Alcott, b. Philadelphia. Author of *Little Women* (1868), which sells millions of copies, sixty thousand in its first year. 1876: Nellie Taylor Ross, b. St. Joseph, Mo. First woman governor, Wyo. (1925–1927). Vice-chair, Democratic National Committee (1928–1932). First woman director, U.S. Mint (1933–1953).

1919: Women are allowed to vote in French elections for the first time. 1924: Shirley Chisholm, b. Brooklyn. First African-American woman elected to Congress (D-N.Y., 1968–1982). First woman and first African-American presidential nominee, Democratic Convention (1972). 1929: Joan Ganz Cooney, b. Phoenix, Ariz. Founder, Children's Television Workshop (1968). "Sesame Street" debuts in 1969 on PBS. 1992: Ann Morrison becomes the first executive editor at *Fortune*, founded 1930. In 1970, an agreement is reached to ensure more promotion opportunities for women. By the end of the seventies, previously all-female research staff is more than half male, and the position is upgraded.

Shirley Chisholm

DECEMBER

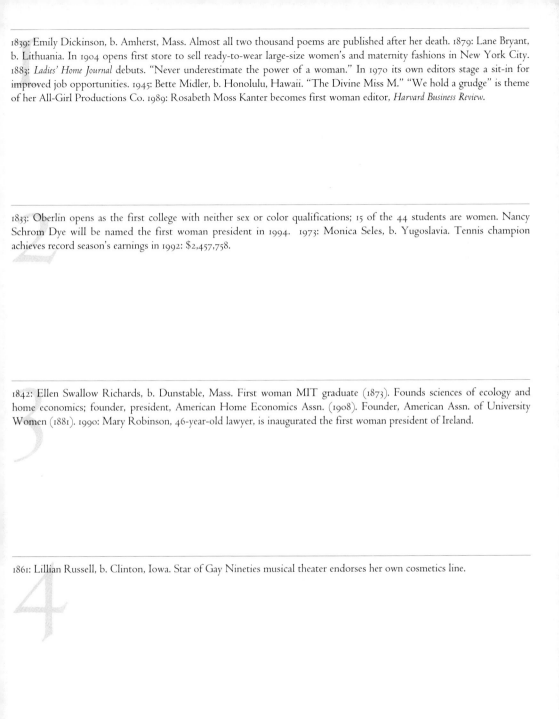

1839: Emily Dickinson, b. Amherst, Mass. Almost all two thousand poems are published after her death. 1879: Lane Bryant, b. Lithuania. In 1904 opens first store to sell ready-to-wear large-size women's and maternity fashions in New York City. 1883: *Ladies' Home Journal* debuts. "Never underestimate the power of a woman." In 1970 its own editors stage a sit-in for improved job opportunities. 1945: Bette Midler, b. Honolulu, Hawaii. "The Divine Miss M." "We hold a grudge" is theme of her All-Girl Productions Co. 1989: Rosabeth Moss Kanter becomes first woman editor, *Harvard Business Review.*

1833: Oberlin opens as the first college with neither sex or color qualifications; 15 of the 44 students are women. Nancy Schrom Dye will be named the first woman president in 1994. 1973: Monica Seles, b. Yugoslavia. Tennis champion achieves record season's earnings in 1992: $2,457,758.

1842: Ellen Swallow Richards, b. Dunstable, Mass. First woman MIT graduate (1873). Founds sciences of ecology and home economics; founder, president, American Home Economics Assn. (1908). Founder, American Assn. of University Women (1881). 1990: Mary Robinson, 46-year-old lawyer, is inaugurated the first woman president of Ireland.

1861: Lillian Russell, b. Clinton, Iowa. Star of Gay Nineties musical theater endorses her own cosmetics line.

1934: Joan Didion, b. Sacramento, Calif. Author, screenwriter. **1935:** Mary McLeod Bethune creates National Council of Negro Women, Washington, D.C. **1956:** Rose Heilbron becomes Britain's first woman judge.

1906: Esther Peterson, b. Provo, Utah. Consumer advocate. Executive vice-chair of the President's Commission on the Status of Women, which she had proposed, in 1961; served under the chairmanship of Eleanor Roosevelt. She successfully lobbied for the Equal Pay Act of 1963, the first federal law against sexual discrimination passed by Congress. **1993:** More women than men are named Rhodes scholars for the first time.

1760: Mme. (Marie Gresholtz) Tussaud, b. Bern, Switzerland. Creates waxwork museum in London. **1893:** Virginia Kirkus, b. Meadville, Pa. In 1933 she launches bimonthly book review service for bookshops. **1936:** Martha Layne Collins, b. Baghdad, Ky. First woman governor, Ky. (1983); chair, Democratic National Convention (1984). **1940:** Carole Simpson, b. Chicago. First African-American woman TV reporter in Chicago (1970); moderates 1992 presidential debate.

1885: Ruth Fanshaw Waldo, b. Scotland, Conn. First VP at J. Walter Thompson advertising agency (1944), supervising women's copy. To distinguish copywriters from secretaries, she establishes tradition of women executives wearing hats. **1916:** Dorothy V. Bush, b. Baldwyn, Miss. First woman officer of major political party: secretary, Democratic party, at 27 (1944–1989).

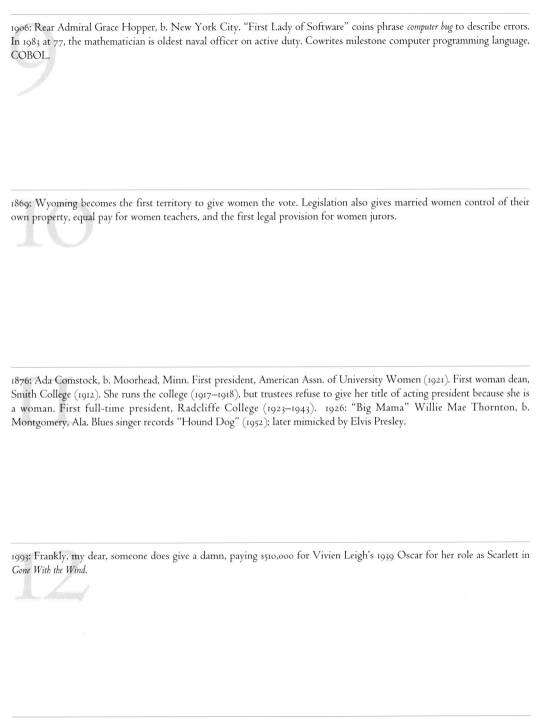

9
1906: Rear Admiral Grace Hopper, b. New York City. "First Lady of Software" coins phrase *computer bug* to describe errors. In 1983 at 77, the mathematician is oldest naval officer on active duty. Cowrites milestone computer programming language, COBOL.

10
1869: Wyoming becomes the first territory to give women the vote. Legislation also gives married women control of their own property, equal pay for women teachers, and the first legal provision for women jurors.

11
1876: Ada Comstock, b. Moorhead, Minn. First president, American Assn. of University Women (1921). First woman dean, Smith College (1912). She runs the college (1917–1918), but trustees refuse to give her title of acting president because she is a woman. First full-time president, Radcliffe College (1923–1943). 1926: "Big Mama" Willie Mae Thornton, b. Montgomery, Ala. Blues singer records "Hound Dog" (1952); later mimicked by Elvis Presley.

12
1993: Frankly, my dear, someone does give a damn, paying $510,000 for Vivien Leigh's 1939 Oscar for her role as Scarlett in *Gone With the Wind*.

1993: Susan A. Maxman becomes the first woman president of the American Institute of Architects in its 135-year history. In 1957, 1% of its members are women; by 1993, they compose 10% of its membership.

1890: *New York Sun* article discusses "why it is our women do not marry" and finds "there are more women qualified to become competent wives than there are men capable of developing into worthy husbands." 1897: Margaret Chase Smith, b. Skowhegan, Maine. First woman nominated for U.S. president by major party, 1964 Republican National Convention. "The Conscience of the Senate." 1961: President's Commission on the Status of Women is established. By 1967, all states have federally mandated women's commissions.

1875: First ad for typists appears in New York City. The hours are shorter than those for shopgirls, with half hour for lunch and higher pay. Initially the women are segregated from male employees.

1485: Catharine of Aragon, b. Spain. First wife of Henry VIII of England. They separate in 1531, after six children die and only one female (Queen Mary) lives. Marriage is annulled so he can marry Anne Boleyn. 1809: Napoleon divorces Josephine because she cannot provide an heir. 1901: Margaret Mead, b. Philadelphia. Anthropologist writes classic text, *Coming of Age in Samoa* (1928). "Try to find something that needs to be done that only you can do." 1941: Lesley Stahl, b. Lynn, Mass. Broadcaster.

1993: Judith Rodin, 49, is named president of Univ. of Pennsylvania, the first woman to head an Ivy League institution.

17

BETTY GRABLE

1916: Betty Grable, b. St. Louis. In 1940s, the actress is highest-paid woman in U.S., earning $300,000 a year.

18

1829: Jane Cunningham Croly, b. England. First syndicated woman's columnist (1857). Founder, Women's Press Club (1889). In that year she organizes General Federation of Women's Clubs. 1939: Cicely Tyson, b. New York City. Actress, wins Emmy for performance in *The Autobiography of Miss Jane Pittman* (1974). Cofounder, Dance Theatre of Harlem. 1974: The National Assn. of Women Business Owners is founded in Washington, D.C. By 1990s, fifty chapters and international affiliates in twenty-eight countries.

20

1865: Elsie de Wolfe, b. New York City. First woman interior decorator; designs Colony Club, New York City's first club for women (1905). 1886: Hazel Hotchkiss Wightman, b. Healdsburg, Calif. Tennis champion wins record forty-four national titles; contributes Wightman Cup; presents the first equal paycheck for women at the U.S. National Championships (1973). When she wears sleeveless dress on court it is revolutionary.

21

1937: Jane Fonda, b. New York City. Oscars: *Klute* (1971); *Coming Home* (1978). Marries Ted Turner on her fifty-fourth birthday. 1954: Chris Evert, b. Ft. Lauderdale, Fla. Wins record of at least one tennis Grand Slam event for twelve consecutive years. 1959: Florence Griffith Joyner, b. Los Angeles. At 1988 Summer Olympics she wins three gold medals and one silver. Cochair, President's Council on Physical Fitness (1993 to the present). Founds FGJ Youth Foundation (1992), Los Angeles.

Florence Griffith Joyner

1912: "Lady Bird" Taylor Johnson, b. Karnack, Tex. First Lady, 1963–1969. First to campaign for husband on her own. Highway Beautification Act of 1965. 1945: Diane Sawyer, b. Glasgow, Ky. In 1994 she will sign unprecedented five-year, $7 million annual contract with ABC News, which gives her three prime-time news programs (1994). Co-anchor, "PrimeTime Live" (1989 to the present). 1993: Two women tennis champions are among the *Forbes* 40 highest-paid athletes: number 15, Steffi Graf, $9.8 million; number 35, Gabriella Sabatini, $6.5 million.

1867: Madame C. J. Walker, b. Delta, La. Orphaned at 6, married at 14, widowed with one daughter at 20, goes on to become the world's first African-American woman millionaire and first self-made American woman millionaire. In 1905, she discovers "hot comb" and hair care formula, which revolutionizes industry. Establishes manufacturing business and marketing distribution system. By 1919, she employs more than twenty-five thousand agents in U.S. and the Caribbean.

1897: "Yes, Virginia, there is a Santa Claus" is the celebrated reply in *The New York Sun* to eight-year-old Virginia O'Hanlon's letter to the editor. 1929: Mary Higgins Clark, b. New York City. Widowed in her 40s, with five children under 13, she publishes first suspense novel in 1975. "My first short story was rejected forty times."

1821: Clara Barton, b. Oxford, Mass. "Angel of the Battlefield" during Civil War. At 60, she founds American Red Cross (1881); president until death (1904). 1889: Lila Acheson Wallace, b. Canada. Cofounder, *Reader's Digest* (1921–1965). At her death in 1984, she is richest woman in U.S., with $250 million. She bequeaths control of the company, worth several billion dollars, to charity. 1954: Margaret Williams, b. Kansas City, Mo. Chief of staff to First Lady Hillary Clinton and the first to be an assistant to the president as well (1993 to the present). 1975: Mary Rodas, b. Englewood, N.J. At 14 she is the youngest corporate VP in U.S.; she earns $200,000 and owns 5% of CATCO, $70 million toy company. National cochair, March of Dimes.

Christmas

Time's "Woman of the Year" have been Wallis Warfield Simpson (1936); Mme. Chiang Kai-shek (with her husband, 1937); Elizabeth II (1952); American Women (1975); and Corazon Aquino (1986).

Boxing Day

1927: Anne L. Armstrong, b. New Orleans. First woman national cochair, Republican Party (1971–1973); first to deliver keynote speech at national convention (1972). 1930: Meg Greenfield, b. Seattle. Pulitzer Prize, Editorial Writing; columnist, *Newsweek*. 1943: Cokie (Boggs) Roberts, b. New Orleans. Radio and TV broadcaster.

Clara Barton

DECEMBER

Elizabeth Arden

28 1918: British women 30 years or older are allowed to vote for the first time. 1967: Muriel Siebert becomes the first woman to own a seat on the N.Y. Stock Exchange. First woman superintendent of banking, N.Y. State (1977).

29 1937: Mary Tyler Moore, b. Brooklyn. "Mary Tyler Moore Show" (1970–1977); head of MTM Enterprises; seven Emmys.

30 1919: First woman law student is admitted to Lincoln's Inn in London.

31 1884: Elizabeth Arden, b. Toronto, Canada. Founder, cosmetics empire, 1900s; her salons' red door becomes signature. 1946: Diane Von Furstenberg, b. Brussels. In her 20s, fashion designer borrows $30,000 and in 1971 introduces the $70 wrap dress. By 1976, *Newsweek* cover story calls her "the most marketable female in fashion since Coco Chanel." In 1993 pioneers designer fashion merchandising on home-shopping television.

New Year's Eve

This book is the culmination of more than a decade of research. Information contained herein was accurate as of January 1994. The foremost challenge was to include as many well-known, as well as unsung, historic and contemporary women leaders around the world as possible and to secure dated facts to suit the daybook format. (Some women did not want their birthdate published.) Another goal was to capture the women's formidable accomplishments in capsule profiles and to chronicle major milestones for women. Choices were made to cover the spectrum of women's progress, including diversity of professions, politics, races, religions, ages, and geography.

Hundreds of resources were consulted to document the data. These included libraries, museums, consulates, government agencies, professional associations, calendars, periodicals, newspapers, reference books, biographies, and the women themselves, some of whom I have had the privilege of working with or knowing. Primary sources included the Woman's Bureau of the U.S. Department of Labor, National Women's History Project, Women's Research and Education Institute (WREI), The Women's Resource Center of New York, Women's Sports Foundation, and the National Women's Hall of Fame. In addition, the *World Almanac*, *Famous American Women*, *Notable American Women*, and the *Book of Women Firsts* were consulted.

Ellen Abrams, Betty-Jean Bavar, Anita Diamant, Judith Gerberg, Cathy Guisewite, Madelyn Jennings, Molly MacGregor, Rep. Carolyn B. Maloney, Abdul Mitha, Mary Murphree, Margaret Richardson, Clara and Irving Stone, Barbara Tober, and Kay Wight were also particularly helpful.

Beverly Wettenstein is a journalist and marketing communications/public affairs executive with *Fortune* 500 corporations and nonprofit associations. She is also an active leader in women's professional and philanthropic organizations and a consultant with the "Take Our Daughters to Work" project. As a volunteer, she spearheaded the New York "Race for the Cure" and initiated the city's bus route sign program. Her honors include recognition in *Who's Who in America*, *Who's Who of American Women*, and *2,000 Notable American Women*.

Picture credits are listed in the order that they appear in each month.

JANUARY
Dorothy Arzner: Culver Pictures
Betsy Ross: The Bettmann Archive
Zora Neale Hurston: Car Van Vechten/Prints and Photographs Division, Library of Congress
Gertrude Vanderbilt Whitney: Culver Pictures
Maya Angelou: © 1993 John Loengard
Ruth St. Denis: Nickolas Muray/National Portrait Gallery, Smithsonian Institution/Art Resource, NY
Virginia Woolf: The Bettmann Archive
Oprah Winfrey: Gwendolen Cates/Sygma

FEBRUARY
Gertrude Stein: The Bettmann Archive
Elizabeth Blackwell: Culver Pictures
Rosa Parks: UPI/Bettmann
Alice Walker: © 1994 Andy Freeberg
Lydia Pinkham: New York Public Library Picture Collection
Leontyne Price: Carl Van Vechten/Prints and Photographs Division, Library of Congress
Suffragettes: Culver Pictures
Marian Anderson: UPI/Bettmann

MARCH
Jackie Joyner-Kersee: Reuters/Bettmann
Sarah Caldwell: Elliott Erwitt/Magnum Photos
Fannie Farmer: The Bettmann Archive
Bella Abzug and Gloria Steinem: UPI/Bettmann
Sarah Vaughan: Frank Driggs Collection
Liz Claiborne: AP/Wide World Photos

APRIL
Jeannette Rankin: UPI/Bettmann
Bette Davis: New York Public Library Picture Collection
Mary Pickford: Prints and Photographs Division, Library of Congress
Clare Boothe Luce: Arnold Genthe/Prints and Photographs Division, Library of Congress
Isak Dinesen: Carl Van Vechten/Prints and Photographs Division, Library of Congress
Charlotte Brontë: Culver Pictures
Dorothea Lange: Prints and Photographs Division, Library of Congress
Coretta Scott King: Lawrence Fried/Magnum Photos

MAY
Billie Jean King: The Bettmann Archive
Martha Graham: The Bettmann Archive
Florence Nightingale: Prints and Photographs Division, Library of Congress
Mary Cassatt: Painting by Edgar Degas/National Portrait Gallery, Smithsonian Institution/Art Resource, NY
Rachel Carson: Erich Hartmann/Magnum Photos
Janet Guthrie: UPI/Bettmann

Mrs. P. F. E. Albee, the first Avon Lady: Courtesy of Avon Products, Inc.
Ida Tarbell: UPI/Bettmann
Katharine Hepburn: Culver Pictures
Abigail Smith Adams: Prints and Photographs Division, Library of Congress
Nellie Bly: UPI/Bettmann
Mary Margaret McBride: The Bettmann Archive
Indira Gandhi: AP/Wide World Photos
Helen Reid: UPI/Bettmann
Shirley Chisholm: UPI/Bettmann

DECEMBER
Lillian Russell: Culver Pictures
Margaret Mead: The Bettmann Archive
Betty Grable: AP/Wide World Photo
Florence Griffith Joyner: Reuters/Bettmann
Clara Barton: Matthew Brady/Prints and Photographs Division, Library of Congress
Elizabeth Arden: Courtesy of Elizabeth Arden Public Relations